The Dead Always Vote Democrat

But Our Troops Don't Get to Vote

By Ben Brink

I0145480

Acknowledgements

This book is dedicated to my wife Janet. The founding Director of American Defense Foundation in 1984, she was responsible for the highly successful Military Voter Registration Drive (MVRP) for the Reagan-Bush campaign in 1984. Her advice and assistance in researching military overseas voting and other aspects of the electoral process was invaluable.

Contents

Introduction

Democracy is two wolves and a lamb voting on what to have for lunch. Liberty is a well-armed lamb contesting the vote.—Ben Franklin[1], 6th President of Pennsylvania[2]

Two life experiences drove me to write this book: a run for Congress in the mid-1990s and my own experience with the ultimate in voter suppression—late and lost overseas military registrations and ballots.

In 1994 I ran for Congress in CA-14, the seat that represented Silicon Valley. A nationally targeted campaign, I won the primary easily against a non-viable candidate with little support and no positions, who just made up things about me. Well, dirty politics is part of the game and most of us believe that liar and politician are just synonymous. However, I expected better in the general—after all, my opponent was a sitting member of Congress. Our internal polling showed that we had pulled close to break-even about 3 ½ weeks before the election. My opponent, Rep. Anna Eshoo, had not expected such a challenger and was in scramble mode to raise money and support at the last minute. Eventually she got about $3M from the DCCC and was able to get a couple of chartered jets of union members, from Chicago I think, to augment her ground game—

all's fair. Did a hard pressed Eshoo campaign resort to vote fraud in that election? I don't think so. But her local postal union was certainly not constrained by the law either. The week before the election some of my campaign staff found thousands of my mailers in the USPS trash bin and the mail that did get through was delivered on or after Election Day. I lost, of course.

It made an impression on me. Dirty politics has always had some success and so is part of the game. Gerrymandered redistricting and election fund-raising laws are biased toward incumbents in both parties. It is annoying and needs to be changed—but it is a process, just like getting the government under control fiscally; and progress is made as people become aware and involved. However, criminal activity such as tampering with the mail and electoral fraud is more than that. It is fundamentally damaging to our democracy because it deprives the people of their most fundamental rights, stifling the people's right to speech and disenfranchising the voter, thus making it impossible for the people to maintain control over their government.

A Navy Captain, now retired after 36 years active and reserve service, I was mobilized and served in Afghanistan during the 2008 US presidential election. My view of that election was unmarred by allegations of ACORN, New Black Panthers, and other unsavory events at home.

Long after I returned I became more and more appalled as I gained awareness of just how bad it really was.

In Afghanistan though, I viewed our election through the eyes of a senior US intelligence officer at ISAF (International Security Assistance Force, the US/NATO-plus coalition) watching the Pakistani election (18 February 2008) and the Afghan Presidential campaign moving up to the Afghan election, which was held after I had come home (20 Aug 2009). I arrived at ISAF in early December 2007; two days after Christmas, 27 December 2007, the lead reform candidate and former prime minister of Pakistan, Benazir Bhutto, was assassinated upon her return from exile. Her death preceded a terribly violent election season, where sometimes hundreds were killed at a time at rallies or in mosques by those that opposed whatever they happened to support. In Afghanistan, the long election season culminated in a horribly fraudulent election, which brought into question the legitimacy of the victorious Hamid Karzai government and has had damaging implications to the progress of the Afghan democracy ever since.

My own experience voting absentee in the US elections from Afghanistan in 2008 was much better than most overseas military voters. I had regular access to the Internet in my job at ISAF (in fact I had had access and separate logins to nine classified and unclassified systems both US and NATO) and, although I travelled extensively, I had an office in Kabul when I was at ISAF. When mobilized I was domiciled in Queen Anne's County, Maryland—that means it was my legal residence for taxation, voting, etc. I was able to request registration and ballot materials by e-mailing the Queen Anne's County Election Commissioner via the NATO unclassified system in my office. The Commissioner sent me a personal e-mail with .pdf copies of all the forms and clear instructions on how to register and request ballot materials and that it could be e-mailed. Once she received them she e-mailed me back a receipt. The ballots themselves arrived with plenty of time and, again, the Commissioner e-mailed me to let me know she had received the ballot in the mail. However, one of my staff, an Army Master Sergeant, had less luck. He lived in Maryland too. However, his county in Maryland, Montgomery, was not as efficient; he used the Federal request card; his ballot was late; and he was able to mail it only 5 days before the election. Neither of us knows if it was ever counted.

While in Afghanistan I was often asked by my Afghan and Pakistani military colleagues how the US was able to conduct clean, non-violent elections even when the populace was sharply divided as it was in 2008 and had been in 2000. Compared to the significant violence and fraud in

Pakistan and Afghanistan, the US certainly looked much better from afar. But as the leading democracy in the world, we really do not do very well. Our system is antiquated and has significant potential for fraud, error, and corruption. We are in the bottom quartile in voter participation among the democracies. Close elections are now regularly decided in the courts. We have a sharply divided populous, the majority of which harbor deep suspicions of our politicians and of the honesty of the vote.

The peaceful order of our society depends on the perception of the legitimacy of the government by the governed. My own electoral experience shows me that politicians will go to great lengths to win an election. And my observation in war shows me that the veneer of civilization is very thin. And so I wrote this little book about election fraud and how to prevent it this year for the election on Tuesday, 6 November 2012.

1. The end justifies the means

Socialists cry "Power to the people", and raise the clenched fist as they say it. We all know what they really mean—power over people, power to the State.—Margaret Thatcher[3], former Prime Minister of the United Kingdom

Democrats believe they take the moral high ground for having a history, dating back to the depression, of electing people they believe are smarter than the rest of us to save us from ourselves. And of course they do that by taking other people's money; other people, who are in their minds, less deserving and certainly less moral than those who work for the Federal Government. Given that self-importance, it is no surprise that the Democratic Party philosophy permits the ends to justify the means. Cheating, ballot stuffing, recounts, etc. are just ways to win the election for the good of the people, whether they voted that way or not.

In the next election, who wins will likely determine the fate of our nation; we will either take a path to larger and more dominant government or a path away from that. We'll be governed by those that believe individuals matter or by those that think the government should tell us what to do, when we should do it, and who should have what. If the people want this, it's one thing; but I'm not just going to sit around and let it happen, engineered by those who would commit election fraud to thwart the will of those people.

Being human enterprises, neither the Republican nor the Democratic parties have the moral right to cast the first stone. Both Republicans and Democrats have stuffed the ballot box; both have bought votes; both have manipulated the count; both have stolen, hidden, or created ballots; and both have passed laws and used lawyers to disenfranchise voters both before and after they have cast their vote.

All that being said, however, it is the Democratic Party that historically uses election fraud as a key and common tool to elect their candidates; it is the Democratic Party that passed and relied upon voter suppression laws such as the poll tax and literacy tests to maintain a century of political control in the South; it is the Democratic Party that created and still runs corrupt political machines in our great cities of Chicago, Boston, Kansas City, St. Louis, New York (until Republican Mayor Fiorello LaGuardia cleaned it up); and it is the Democratic Party that has used every method they could find to disenfranchise overseas military; simply because soldiers, sailors, airmen, and marines vote more Republican than the population at large.

For the Democrats to claim that election fraud is a myth is disingenuous at the very least. For Democrats to twist Republican demands for real voters and clean voter rolls into voter suppression is absurd. It is this authors' belief that Democrat resistance hides a more sinister purpose. Highly inaccurate voter rolls stuffed with felons, non-citizens, duplicates, and the dead enable fraud. Lack of positive Voter ID further enables it.

History shows that election fraud has existed in American elections since before the Revolution. However, even if it didn't, the potential for fraud is enough to demand that measures be taken to prevent it. In endeavors where integrity is necessary to engender confidence, law and regulation exists to reduce the possibility of malfeasance and fraud. Consider banking, investments, medicine, food, consumer goods. All are highly regulated to protect citizens' rights and welfare. Why should elections be different? Government reflecting the will of the people is the most fundamental of American rights, and ensuring this was one of the fundamental reasons for our Revolution. It is as important now as then and the perception that our officials were elected fair and square is vital to the legitimacy of our government. Election fraud exists; but whether it did or not, ensuring that it does not is vital to the continuation of our republic.

But this can be fixed. Honorable men and women of both parties have advocated reforms such as accurate voter rolls and Voter ID, including Democrats such as former President Jimmy Carter, whose own early experience fighting corruption and election fraud in Georgia, made him a crusader for fair and fraud-free elections throughout his public life.

2. Vote fraud, a primer

Those who cast the votes decide nothing. Those who count the votes decide everything.—Josef Stalin[4], General Secretary Communist Party USSR

It is a Democratic Party talking point that vote fraud is so uncommon in the United States that actions to reduce the opportunity to commit fraud are unnecessary, wasteful, and a smokescreen to suppress certain classes from voting. The argument is often made that because a reduction in vote fraud has generally been favorable to Republican candidates, those who advocate it must be advocating some sort of fraud themselves.

I will show later in this book that there is sufficient evidence of historical vote fraud, registration fraud, and manipulation of the vote by party operatives, a majority of which have been members of the Democratic Party, that the first argument is simply wrong. However, even if there were not historical evidence of fraud, the damage that the perception of a dirty election can do the legitimacy of government is significant and undesirable. Further, enacting law to reduce the possibility of fraud and increase in other endeavors is considered acceptable by the Democrats; regulation of such industries as banking and the financial markets, even where fraud has not been a problem, is tight—just to prevent the possibility. Shouldn't we be as equally protected in the guarantee of the validity of our vote as we choose those who represent us? After all a main cause of our Revolution was lack of representation. If our vote is diluted and the will of the majority is thwarted by fraudulent elections, then do we not have the same issue today?

Democrats argue that actions to ensure fraud-free elections must be a partisan Republican activity simply because fraud-free elections generally favor Republicans. It is a backwards argument—eliminating fraud only favors Republicans if Democrats have been committing the fraud; and it appears that that has been the case. The Democrats protest too much and make a non-credible argument.

In September 2005, a bipartisan commission chaired by former President Carter and Secretary of State Baker recommended Voter ID as being an important factor in reducing vote fraud. The Supreme Court upheld an Indiana Voter ID law, which provided free IDs for those that did not have them, to be reasonable and acceptable. It is reasonable to require a voter to be who s/he says s/he is—this is required to buy things, travel, bank, obtain food stamps, and travel abroad as a U.S citizen. Why is it too much of a burden to prove you are who you say you are to execute the fundamental and extremely important requirement of voting? After all, those who vote without the right to do so lessen the right to vote of those, who are entitled. And those, who vote without the right, unrightfully make a claim on the property of those affected by their votes. It is theft of our liberty and of our property.

Democrats argue that removing aliens from the voter rolls in states such as Florida and Texas discriminate against Hispanics. But since in those states, most aliens registered are Hispanics, one would expect that most alien registrations removed would also have Hispanic names—the Democrats love confusing correlation with causality and independent variables with dependent ones.

Similarly the Democrats argue that removing old, obsolete, registrations—such as the dead and multiple registrations—discriminate; but how? Should the dead be allowed to vote? And since on average most dead are older than most living, does removing their names discriminate against old people? No, of course it does not.

But old, outdated, alien, dead, and felon registrations are exactly those registrations useful to those who would cheat—because it is improbable (or in the case of the dead, impossible) for them to vote on their own and so their registrations are available to be used by an impersonator. And since the DOJ has through unilateral action delayed Voter ID in many states, those spare registrations can be voted by anybody, without any evidence that fraud had taken place.

So the Democrats would claim that having to prove who you are and having to be actually alive are unreasonable voter suppression techniques used by the nasty Republicans to keep old, homeless, and illegals from voting. Shame on us—those voters would probably vote Democrat. They would definitely vote Democrat if voted by a Democrat poll worker or campaign volunteer.

But the Democrats are unapologetic about real voter suppression of a class of Americans that are reliable Republican majority—overseas military voters. Historically, and decreasing recently, only a small percentage (4.6% in 2010 according to the Military Voter Protection Project[5]) of overseas military voters—those who defend the ramparts of our nation in the cesspits of the earth—receive their registrations and ballots in time to return their votes in time to be counted on Election Day. And most of the states and counties that are late sending ballots historically have what—they have Democrat election commissioners, of course.

3. Democrats cry foul, again

A lie told often enough becomes the truth —
Vladimir Lenin[6], First Premier USSR

To misquote the Beatles, "imagine there's no vote fraud, it isn't hard to do, No dead people out there voting, and no miscounting too." Well, the Democrats' oft-spoken claim that vote fraud is a myth and that Republicans use it to justify efforts to suppress the votes to disenfranchise minorities and the poor is just as silly. In particular the Democrats suggest that the occurrences of vote fraud are so few that fixing it need not be a priority and, as such, the expense is too high to resolve.

It is certainly interesting that Democrats, not known for their fiscal restraint, are always the first to trot out expense as a reason not to do something they oppose. In reality, the US currently has a very expensive voting system—more than 10 times more costly per voter than Canada's—with highly inaccurate voter rolls, antiquated voting systems, inaccurate counting methodologies, insecure voting systems, and lack of audit trails.[7]

But let's first start with the claim that there is little or no "voter fraud", the term the Democrat's like, or more accurately, "electoral fraud" or "vote fraud" (the term used in this book), which includes not only fraudulent voting but also fraudulent registration, voter intimidation, holding polls open until the desired candidate gets enough votes, ballot manipulation, vote miscounting, crooked judges, felons as poll workers, and, if all those fail, frivolous lawsuits.

Assume there is no electoral fraud. There is, however, the perception among most Americans that laws are needed to prevent electoral fraud. In fact, according to a recent Fox News poll, 70 percent of Americans believe that "Voter ID laws are needed to stop illegal voting." An overwhelming 87 percent of Republicans believe so, along with 74 percent of independents; even a 52 percent majority of Democrats agree. And 50 percent of Americans believe that those opposing Voter ID are doing so in bad faith.[8]

Since the legitimacy of a free government depends upon a belief by the people that elections are fair; the fact that a significant majority believes that the electoral process is tainted should alone be enough to argue for the implementation of laws and systems to ensure fair elections. But consider also that laws and regulations to create the perception of fairness and transparency are commonplace in other areas of our society. As an example, in the financial industry regulation exists to prevent fraud or the perception of fraud. These regulations exist both to protect investors but, as should be with elections, to maintain the perception of legitimacy of the financial markets. Without the perception of honest markets the financial system would falter, so laws and regulations have been put in place to prevent the opportunity to commit fraud, even where it has been uncommon, because the alternative would permanently damage market confidence and, as a result, the national and world economy.

I will present numerous recent and historical examples of Democratic Party registration and electoral fraud, but let's continue now with the assumption that there is not a lot of detected fraud. In fact the claim is made by Democrats that the number is less than 0.2 percent. But, as of June 2011, the total number of registered voters was 178 Million—so 0.2 percent was about 356,000 votes—a very large number in close elections such as Florida in 2000, where the Democrats efforts to destroy, disallow, or disqualify votes for Bush, whittled the margin of victory to 172 before the Supreme Court stepped in and stopped the process. So even so called small amounts of electoral fraud can have large impact.

So, if the perception of fair elections is necessary for the legitimacy of government, and there exists evidence of fraud or deliberate election modification (if you prefer something more politically correct), how might it occur, to whom does it give advantage, and how might it be reduced or eliminated?

There are a lot of registrations that are old, obsolete, and just plain wrong. Of the 177 million registrations in the US, a little over one percent of those registered are dead, and nearly two percent are registered in at least two states. [9] That is about five million registrations that could be used fraudulently. How? In states without Voter ID, pretty much anyone could walk in, claim to be someone they knew were unlikely to vote, and vote themselves.

How can the rolls be fixed? Conduct regular computer comparison and purges of the dead against the Social Security death index and local death records and the use of commercial software to highlight and remove duplicate registrations that haven't been voted in an election cycle. For good measure, require government-issued Voter ID to ensure that voters are who they say they are. How can it be ensured that a purge doesn't disenfranchise someone in error? Allow provisional voting for someone that claims a purge was made in error. This is exactly what many states have already done to comply with the Help America Vote Act (HAVA), a Federal law passed in 2002, which among other things establishes standards for maintaining accurate voter registration rolls.

In response, President Obama's Justice Department has engaged in a frenzy of lawsuits against the states like Florida and Arizona to stop or slow down the registration clean-up process. Finally in June, the courts ruled against the Fed's attempts to thwart Florida's efforts to clean up the voter rolls and Department of Homeland Security released data from the Systematic Alien Verification for Entitlements (SAVE)[10] so Florida could complete the job in time for the November election.

The claim has been that a purge of voter rolls discriminates against poor, in particular Hispanic and African American, Democrats—presumably because the poor move more often and don't know to re-register or are afraid to because they are on the lam. No doubt, the claim will eventually be made that purging the dead discriminates against old people because they are close to death. The claim is also made that Voter ID discriminates against the poor, presumably because Democrats believe they are too stupid or too lazy to pick up a free Voter ID card. Unfortunately for the Justice Department, statistics just don't support this insulting position and, in states with Voter ID, registrations and percent voting among poor and minorities have gone up.

4. Yes Virginia, there really is election fraud

But, in the end, truth will out.—William Shakespeare[11], Playwright

The Democrats contend that there is no vote fraud. However, even if there weren't any fraud, the opportunity for fraud is significant enough, and the importance of free and fair elections is important enough, and the US management of election is poor enough that we must implement safeguards such as regularly updated voter rolls and voter id.

But there is vote fraud, there has always been vote fraud, and there is a certainty that there will always be vote fraud. And the Democratic Party and their servants, the unions, have a long and sordid history stretching back more than a century and a half of using vote fraud to get their way. The end will justify the means.

While there are certainly examples of Republican vote fraud it is historically less common than Democrat. For Republicans it is usually local and not strategically core to the party's efforts to win national elections. Republican election manipulations are usually before the fact, and in concert with Democrats of like mind—gerrymandering, a sin of both parties;

and voter discouragement—neither illegal but both certainly unsavory.

Electoral fraud comes in several flavors. In addition to fraud, there are other, legal ways that the vote is manipulated—a couple of which were causes of the American Revolution—to assure that party candidates triumph over the will of the people. First, let's look at things that are fraudulent today:

Voting for another. This is the act of voting for another person, such as an invalid, that cannot vote themselves. The helper goes to the poll with the invalid voter and actually votes for them—in a manner that may not agree with the desire of the voter. This is a nearly undetectable crime in a nation of secret ballots. However, there are many stories, usually from claims made by the helper that this happens regularly. It is unquantifiable to determine the size of the problem and it is probably not fixable unless and until voting machines allow voice voting.

Voting for the dead; and for the moved. There are about 1.8 million dead that are still registered in this country and 2.8 million with registrations in two or more states. It is likely that there are many more with more than one registration in the same state. Voting for these unlikely-to-be-used registrations is very easy and with little risk in a state without Voter ID.

Based on lack of convictions, Democrats insist substitution fraud occurs seldom if ever. However, it is a nearly undetectable crime. Unless more than one person tries to vote the same unused registration, fraudulent use of that registration is likely not to be detected. If, for some reason, such use is detected then it would never be prosecuted by a winner that benefits; the loser seldom has the resources of government to pursue the matter; and except in a close election where the difference might affect the outcome, it is hard to get anyone to care.

Nonetheless, the potential for dead/moved vote fraud is tremendous. The number of excess/obsolete registrations is enough to change the outcome of nearly any election. Prevention is easy—cull the voter rolls of these registrations and require Voter ID to make sure a voter is who he or she says he is. The Democrats vehemently oppose this. The only logical reason for their opposition is because it curtails a beneficial and long used tool to win elections for Democrats.

Purchasing votes. There are numerous historical stories of giving inducement to vote in elections. Prior to secret ballots and laws prohibiting it, drink and food were given in return for voting the right way. In fact, in ancient Rome it was called *ambitus* or "canvass support"; that is where the English word "ambitious" comes from. Julius Caesar was famous for it. In America, before the founding of the Republic, buying votes with booze was known as "swilling the planters with bumbo". In his first race for the Virginia House of Burgesses in 1758, George Washing bought 160 gallons of rum, bear, wine, and cider to encourage his 391 voters.[12] This was a major way that elections in ancient Rome and Colonial America were won—the candidate, who could give the best gifts and throw the best events emerged the victor on Election Day. Of course Julius Caesar and Washington both had reputations for honor and such things were legal back then. But today, buying a vote is fraudulent.

But does it still go on? Well yes it does. In fact Fox News reported on 29 July 2012 that drug dealers in Eastern Kentucky routinely paid $25/vote for local officials such as Sheriffs. Richard Moore, a local resident, explained that he had sold 4 votes for Michael Salyers a candidate for county magistrate, currently cooling his heels in jail for vote buying, and was paid $100. Moore told the reporter that "just about everybody sells votes." A US attorney for the Eastern District of Kentucky, Kerry Harvey, revealed that in Clay County, over $400,000 was spent to buy 8,00votes for $50 each; he suspects drug money.[13]

Registration fraud. This kind of fraud is perpetrated by third party organizations, such as the infamous ACORN, that solicit people to register to vote. Sometimes even dogs and dead people are registered to vote. The point of registration fraud is twofold: to legitimize voting by those without the legal right to vote, such as aliens and felons; and to create likely unused registrations that can be voted fraudulently if necessary to win. How can this be fixed: first, compare registrations against the legal status of voters; second, require a Voter ID, which to get requires the certification of the hopeful voter's eligibility to vote.

Voter suppression. The biggest historical case of voter suppression, of course, were the Jim Crow laws, which set requirements, such as literacy tests and poll taxes, that made it difficult for poor whites and African Americans in the South to become eligible to vote. The Democrats like to call any new voter law proposed by Republicans to reduce election fraud "new Jim Crow laws". But this rewrites history, for these laws were the creation of white southern Democrats that lasted from the end of the Reconstruction until the Congress and Courts finally ended it in the mid-1960s. These laws tried to disenfranchise legitimate voters through things like poll taxes and literacy tests, and, in some states the military. However, Democrats today, try to twist the truth and cry "Jim Crow" and "Voter suppression!" to condemn any effort to reduce inaccuracies in the voter rolls or require positive identification of a voter.

Real, modern voter suppression consists of three primary things: voter confusion; voter intimidation; and voter disenfranchisement.

Voter confusion: Example: in the 2000 Bush v. Gore race, Democrats and the press told voters in the Florida Panhandle that the polls had closed an hour before they actually did. The reason: the Panhandle was on Central Time and the rest of Florida on Eastern Time, polls had an hour more to go. Estimates are that this may have cost President Bush over 10,000 votes.

Example: in the 2012 Congressional primary between Representative Charlie Rangel and challenger State Senator Andriano Espaillat primary in New York, supporters of Espaillat claimed that signs had been set up misdirecting voters from the polling places and poll workers had told voters they were not able to vote in the district. Yes, the Democrats will use shenanigans even against their own.

Voter Intimidation: Example: in 2008, armed New Black Panther Party Obama supporters intimidated Clinton voters in Philadelphia during the Pennsylvania primary as well as poll watchers during the general election. The Bush administration Department of Justice began investigations against the New Black Panther's, which were summarily dropped once

Obama took office. The New Black Panthers were back intimidating again during the 2010 elections

Voter inconvenience: The Democrats complain that Voter ID is a method of voter suppression because it may discourage the poor from going through the effort of voting. However, in states that have implemented Voter ID, both registrations and turnout have increased, especially for minority voters. In Georgia, the first state to implement Voter ID in 2006, registrations and voter turnout have increased significantly more for minority voters than for whites.

Ballot manipulation: Numerous examples exist throughout recent history of lost and found ballots, late ballots, and modified ballots: remember Florida 2000, when Democrat poll workers double punched ballots to ensure a Gore vote and/or bad ballot while driving a circuitous route from the polls to the county election offices. From the Kennedy Nixon election of 1960 to the Wisconsin recall election of 2012, ballot boxes disappeared for a time and then reappeared at just the right time, sometimes with more ballots than registered votes, and unexpectedly with just enough votes in favor of a Democratic candidate to ensure victory. This and absentee ballot manipulation may be the most common, and undetectable kind of vote fraud—and a regular tactic of the Democrat election ground game.

Absentee ballot fraud: Examples abound of thousands of voted absentee ballots being found in the trash after pickup from the Post Office. There are even more stories of helpers voting absentee ballots at retirement homes. Stories abound of absentee ballots being kept in unguarded rooms. And the greatest opportunity for voter suppression is late-mailed absentee ballots sent to our overseas troops. Little supervision, a long time between voting and counting, and a lack of chain of custody provides the hopeful Democratic Party worker with many opportunities for manufactured victory.

5. Old, wrong, or dead—enabling election fraud

Unfortunately, the United States has a long history of voter fraud that has been documented by historians and journalists.—John Paul Stevens, Associate Justice, US Supreme Court[14]

Chicago Tribune writer, Andrew Gumbel, asked former President Jimmy Carter what would happen if the Carter Center international election monitoring team turned its focus on the United States instead of another nation. Carter said that the Carter Center would never agree to monitor a US election. "We wouldn't think of it"..."The American political system wouldn't measure up to any sort of international standards." Not surprising, Gumbel writes, "The Chicago Tribune, a paper that knows its vote fraud, having won a Pulitzer for work on the infamous Daley Machine, found 118,000 dead people on the registration lists of six key battleground states."[15]

The Pew Center on the States has followed voting these kinds of voting issues for some time. In early 2012, Pew issued a study it had commissioned MIT to conduct that revealed voter registration and election systems "plagued with errors and inefficiencies that waste taxpayer dollars, undermine voter confidence, and fuel partisan disputes over the integrity of our elections."[16] The issues revealed in this report were not little things and the potential for casting doubt upon the legitimacy of US elections, or indeed the opportunity for outright fraud, are immense.

Over 24 percent of US citizens eligible to vote are unregistered—that is at least 51 million people. Contrast this to Canada, where over 95 percent of citizens[17] are registered to vote. And, despite federal requirements in National Voter Registration Act (NVRA and also called Motor Voter) as amended by the Help America Vote Act (HAVA), passed in 2002 and the Military and Overseas Empowerment Act (MOVE), passed in 2009, not all states yet maintain, or have even entered, all registered voters in a centralized database. In many areas, registrations are still maintained by the counties and are inconsistent throughout an individual state. Campaigns attempting to access and download voter files, which they are allowed to do by law, find in many areas that it is expensive and hard to do—giving a structural advantage to incumbents over lesser experienced or funded challengers.

The PEW study went on to reveal that approximately 24 Million of voter registrations on the books were significantly inaccurate or no longer valid. Of those 24 Million, 1.8 Million were dead. This number is less than the margin of victory for four presidential elections in the past

23

58 years: 1960 Kennedy/Nixon 0.1 Million; 1968 Nixon/Humphrey .5 Million; 1976 Carter/Ford 1.7 Million; 2000 Bush/Gore -0.5 Million; and only slightly greater in 2004 Bush/Kerry 3.0 Million.[18] More tellingly, in a majority of elections in the past six decades, the margin of victory in key battleground states has been less than the number of dead voters in those states.

The report had more on inaccuracies. Approximately 2.76 Million people had registrations in more than one state. In fact, 1,807 were registered in more than three states, 68,725 in three, and 2,688,046 in two.

To achieve this incredibly superb level of accuracy, the US spends $4-7.50/year to register and maintain each registration, compared to Canada, which spends about $0.41 per voter[19]. Canada maintains significantly more accurate registration rolls, for a larger percent of the voting population, and has an internationally superb reputation for an almost non-existent incidence of election fraud.

The report goes on to discuss reasons for the inaccuracies—primary among them are: no access to modern data-matching techniques regularly used in private industry; reactive policies—responding to third party organizations rather than regular internal procedures; and dealing with corrections in paper format, which much be entered into the databases. More recently, in the current election cycle, add that the federal government is refusing to provide data required by law. In Florida's attempt to clean the voter rolls of aliens and those that have moved, Department of Homeland Security, apparently for partisan reasons, refused for months to pass its data on aliens (not just illegal) living in the US but not entitled to vote. Until June 2012, the state was forced to use much less accurate Department of Motor Vehicle records to try to attempt the same thing. Even worse, Obama's Department of Justice sued to block some states such as Florida from using the Social Security Death index to cull the dead from the voter rolls— an obvious, simple, and reasonable thing to do.

Suffice it to say that that the registration rolls in the US are a complete mess. Interestingly they appear to be significantly worse in counties and states controlled by Democrats. Hmm, I wonder why.

Whether fraud exists or not, inflated and inaccurate voter rolls raise the specter of potential fraud. Combined with the vitriolic Democratic Party resistance to the use of Voter ID and a sordid, fraud-laden history in some Democrat machine-run cities, this raises the reasonable suspicion by Republicans that there is fraudulent intent. And with those suspicions, comes the question of legitimacy of any government elected in such a system. Was George Bush elected in 2000? Most studies after the fact confirm that he was, but the question affected his ability to govern at least until 9/11 rallied the nation around its Commander in Chief.

Our political leaders should not have to deal with this. There is enough of importance that must be dealt with in our nation's government that questions of legitimate elections should not be one of an elected leader's problems—no matter what their party. And we the people must not only demand that it be fixed but, until it is, we must volunteer our time to ensure fair and fraud-free elections, in which all those entitled to vote may do so without intimidation, but in which no others may vote. How? See the final chapter.

6. Registration fraud—examples, lots of examples

History is Philosophy teaching by examples.—Thucydides[20], Greek historian

Tim Morris received registration materials for his dead dog, Mo (Mozart), in June 2012, from the Voter Participation Center; an advocacy group opposed to Voter ID laws (I wonder why).

The reason they could do this was a gap in the election laws—that the Democrats blamed the Republicans for, of course—allowing registration by mail. Now here is the key—they really didn't care if their registered voters actually voted. They cared that these unlikely voters made it possible for others to vote for them. Even for poor old Mozart—without an ID, who would know that the dog that showed up on Election Day wasn't the right bitch. Bark if you've voted for Obama! Hope and change, baby! And maybe some Beggin' strips—dogs don't know it's not bacon![21]

Well, this is what the 2012 election is going to be about; real living American voters—too many of them Republican—vs. Dead Dogs for Obama. And they're suing everybody and his brother to keep those voter rolls stuffed with contingency votes.

Shortly after the Mo story, similar stories were released about Scampers, a live Virginia cat and probably a Libertarian that also received the forms. Both animals had their names preprinted on the forms. In a similar story, it was revealed a few days later that a dog was registered in New Mexico, alive this time.[22]

The dead can vote in New Hampshire. During the January 2012 Primary in New Hampshire, James O'Keefe's Project Veritas continued its effort to document the ease with which those intent on committing fraud could request and vote ballots for the dead. In a film taken at that time, several volunteers went into the polls and requested ballots for still-registered dead, not by claiming they were those people but by simply asking for the ballot. In all but one case, where the poll worker actually knew the deceased, the ballot was turned over without question. According to New Hampshire law, no ID is necessary to vote. Intent on committing no crime, the volunteers immediately returned the ballots and told the poll workers what they were doing. No laws were broken and no ballots voted.[23]

Voting for others in DC. In a test at the Washington DC primary early in 2012, a volunteer for Project Veritas asked and received Attorney General Eric Holder's ballot. I presume that they didn't vote the ballot and gave it back although it wasn't confirmed in the article.

Holder, of course, has been blocking every effort by the states to implement vote fraud safeguards such as Voter ID, which would have rendered the test unsuccessful.[24]

More voters than people in Virginia. June 20, 2012: according the most recent US Census, Lincoln County West Virginia has 19,595 registered voters and 16,790 people over 18.[25] Who could those extra 2,895 or 16.7 percent of the voting age population possible be?

Massachusetts Registration. In August 2012 the US Senator Scott Brown vs. Elizabeth Warren race has a new issue. This is not exactly fraud, but illustrates the Democrats strategy to stuff the registration rolls not only with likely Democratic voters but also with registrations not likely to be voted. In response to a Democratic suit demanding greater a court case based on Motor Voter, the State of Massachusetts is providing $270,000 to mail voter registration cards to welfare recipients, who may not have received them then they visited a Department of Transitional Assistance to pick up their welfare check. Brown has challenged the policy, "I want every legal vote to count, but it's outrageous to use taxpayer dollars to register welfare recipients as part of a special effort to boost one political party over another," the Senator said in a statement on Wednesday. "This effort to sign up welfare recipients is being aided by Elizabeth

Warren's daughter, and it's clearly designed to benefit her mother's political campaign."[26] Is it fraud? No. Is it abuse of public funds targeted to aid a Democratic Party Candidate? Maybe! Does it enable fraud on Election Day? Definitely!

Florida works to remove dead voters. In 2012, the State of Florida instructed its county election commissioners to remove approximately 53,000 registered voters also appearing on the Social Security Death Index. County officials cannot just remove the names but must either be presented with a death certificate, which they evidently don't have easy access to in a state database, or send out a letter, wait a month, and , if there is no reply, then remove the voters.[27]

The dead vote in California and every place else, evidently. The dead walk, or vote, among us. In 2008, a California Bay Area TV station did a study, finding that 232 people with death certificates had voted—some more than once; 135 were from Alameda County. In Connecticut 8,500 dead people remained on the list; Florida found 65,000 ineligible and duplicate voters as well as 6,000 dead; Madison County, Mississippi had more than 123% registered voters than people over the age of 18 and 486 of those were over 105; and Rhode Island had no law to remove dead voters; Dallas County Texas found 6,000 dead voters and Harris county found 4,000. In 2006 New York new electoral database

30

identified 77,000 of the still voting dead; the Tennessee State Senate nullified the election of Ophelia Ford after learning that two poll workers had cast votes for her, including two that were dead. [28] Most recently, a new Pew study found that there are at least 1.8 million dead voters nationwide. Obama's Department of Justice took legal action earlier in 2012 to slow the purge of these voters, but the process is ongoing in many states and Florida won a recent lawsuit permitting the effort to proceed just before the publishing of this book.

Proof of illegals on voter rolls. In 2005 the Government Accountability Office (GAO) did a random audit of US District court records to look at fall out of non-citizens from jury calls. In the federal courts, jury members are called from voter registration rolls. Approximately 3 percent, or 900, of the 30,000 individuals called were found to be ineligible as jurors because they were not citizens. There is indisputable evidence that aliens, both legal and illegal are registering and voting in elections. Whether this is the result of fraud or just a misunderstanding of the law, it is illegal and effectively disenfranchises citizens actually qualified to vote. While three percent may not seem like a large number, in a close election it can make the difference in who wins. Nationwide, 3 percent is approximately 5.3

31

Million voters—more than the margin of victory in two of the last five presidential elections.

In 1996, incumbent Republican US Representative Bob Dornan lost to Democratic challenger Loretta Sanchez. Sanchez won the election by 979 votes and Dornan contested it to the House of Representatives. The committee found 624 ballots voted by legal aliens documented by the INS that had applied, but not been granted citizenship, and another 124 improper absentee ballots. However, illegal aliens not documented by the INS would not be detected. As the Oversight Committee pointed out, "If there is a significant number of 'documented aliens,' aliens in INS records, on the Orange County voter registration rolls, how many illegal or undocumented aliens may be registered to vote in Orange County?". Given that the margin of victory was only 231 at that point, it is clearly possible that Dornan lost the election through votes of those in this country illegally.[29]

Opposition to Voter ID. In August 2000 an anti-Voter ID forum was held in Minneapolis. In the meeting, Chairman Rep. Keith Ellison (DFL-state Democrat affiliate-MN), claimed that Voter ID would be so costly as to cause the streets not to be plowed in Ramsey County. His Republican challenger, Chris Fields challenged the costs as being made up and that such inflated rhetoric caused Voter ID opponents to lose all credibility.

"What disturbs me is some of the rhetoric coming from the other side, saying this is a poll tax," he said. "That's completely disingenuous, to say the least. We're not telling folks they can't vote. We're not putting up a barrier between them and their right to vote. We just want to make sure that the integrity of our electoral system is sound."[30]

National Voter Registration Act of 1993 The NVRA also known as the Motor Voter Act, was signed into law by President Clinton in 1993. The act was a compromise that required states to make available voter registration material to a potential qualified voter at offices where they applied for or renewed drivers' licenses or social services but also that required states to update and scrub voter rolls on a regular basis.[31] The bill had some negative outcomes in that it facilitated some fraudulent registrations but some good outcomes in that it enabled easier registration—although voter turnout has actually declined since the passage of the bill. Combined with amendments in the Help America Vote Act (HAVA), which clarified minimum election administration standards, the bill provides the legal basis for States to purge voter rolls of obsolete, duplicate, illegal, and dead voters currently being interfered with by Obama's Department of Justice.

Same Day registration is seen by its proponents as the next positive step in creating open and fair elections. The rosy picture that is painted of same day registration is that it allows *everyone* to participate. Opponents of same day registration will argue that the downside to same day registration is that it allows *everyone* to participate! The nuance is whether the voters are legally entitled to vote or not. The whole idea of registering to vote when moving to a new community or even when getting a driver's license apparently was neither fast enough nor convenient enough for those poor souls about to sit out an election due to their own procrastination. It was also too large a voting block for liberals and progressives to allow staying home and not voting. Stuart Comstock-Gay Director of Democracy Program is quoted by Mannix Porterfield in the West Virginia Register Herald "surveys have shown that same-day registration increases voter turnout, particularly among younger voters. "You can typically expect a 5-6 percent increase in turnout. And once people vote a first time, they are 80 percent more likely to vote again."[32]

Same Day registration is not a new idea. It's the recurring brainchild of liberals and progressives who have been systematically trying to convert states to their way of thinking for years. It's been tried before and tossed out as unworkable in Oregon. That state dropped same day registration in 1986, instead going to a twenty day voter registration cutoff prior to the election. Oregon also chose to vote by mail. The Oregonian editorial board encouraged more: "Oregon's turnout is consistently good. But it could be much better with same day registration."

But the process carries too much risk for mischief and ignores the eligibility validation and fact checking required to be done at the polls. It has a nasty reputation for double registrations and double voting by college students registered both at home, and at their school—on Election Day. The risk of fraud was evidently too much for voters in California and Colorado in 2000, where same day registration was on the ballot in both states. The measure was soundly defeated by approximately 60-40 percent margins.

Crush of New Voter Registrations, 2008. According to a report put out by the generally progressive Brennan Center for Justice, "New York's registration system urgently needs reform. Under the current, outdated system, election clerks process mountains of paper forms that voters submit—often at the last minute before the registration deadline, which can swamp officials at the very time they need to be preparing for Election Day." [33]

Robert Bauer and Trevor Potter wrote in the Washington Post, addressing the last minute voter registration crush. The problem they assert is the "near exclusive reliance on paper voter registration forms." It seems everyone is frustrated by the registration process that is in effect. Millions of Americans are made ineligible due to filling out the paper form illegibly, incorrectly or having the ballots read or recorded by the voter registration officials incorrectly. Meanwhile the potential for fraud such as duplicate voting remains high and mountains of paper voter registration forms make it all the more difficult to guard against.[34]

Bev Harris of Black Box Voting.org, found that in 2008 "last minute dumps of new voter registration forms was a national problem" For instance, voter registration in Memphis was severely hobbled by the influx of voter registration forms. "In Memphis, approximately 30,000 new registration forms flowed in during the last five weeks before the 2008 presidential election. Only half of these [registered voters] made it onto the voter list by the start of early voting. While the 2008 presidential election brought millions of new voters to the polls, Black Box Voting found that third party registration groups possibly failed in their "fiduciary-like duty to the voter", whom Harris says "has every reason to believe they will be registered timely after signing forms and entrusting them to a responsible person."[35]

Stuart Comstock-Gay is a community organizer and voting rights advocate, formerly with DEMOS and the National Voting Rights Institute. He wrote about New Jersey in the days before the November 2008 Presidential election in a piece for the Huffington Post, "in New Jersey, it seems the crush of new voter registrations forms has so overwhelmed election offices in some counties that the registrations have not yet been processed, and some thousands of people are going to the polls finding that they are not in the official book. Morris County alone says they have a backlog of 1500 registration forms." [36]

Bauer and Potter's belief that paper voter registration forms are outdated is supported by HAVA. That act created standards to assist states in centralizing the voter registration lists into a single database. Bauer and Potter recommend that a few steps still need to be done to build an efficient and modern voting infrastructure. They propose that a paperless voter registration done by the state, which automatically identifies and registers voters, takes the burden away from the individual voter and eliminates the need for the unreliable independent voter registration organization. Taking that single step eliminates the "last minute deluge of registration activity that consumes election officials and addresses the risks of registration fraud." Finally, they conclude, "there should be fail-safe mechanisms—online and offline—for voters to securely update and correct information and vote on Election Day.[37]

Comstock-Gay's suggested approach is similar, albeit perhaps more heavy handed reliance upon the power of the federal government rather than the state. "Ultimately, we simply must get to the international standard of universal and permanent registration. If the government had an affirmative obligation to get everybody registered, these problems could go away."[38]

Fewer people voting—not just in the US. It is true that all citizens should be encouraged to register and to vote. It is also true that US voter turnout historically is slowly declining and now hovering between 50-55 percent in Presidential elections[39]. With an occasional spike in interest, such as in 2008, US voting is near the bottom of developed countries that do not have compulsory voting (e.g. Netherlands and Australia). There are a number of factors for the low voting percentages, including demographics such as the multicultural and multilingual nature of the American population as well as the younger age and mobility of Americans. In addition, negative advertising and the polarization of the political process is seen as a factor.[40]

To put this in perspective, our neighbor Canada has also shown a decline in voter turnout from the mid-70s a decade or so to high 58-61 percent in the last two elections.[41] In fact, all western democracies have shown a decrease in voter turnout but also in participation in political parties and in general civic participation in such things as church participation, professional societies, youth groups, and parent teacher associations. Globally, voter turnout has decreased on the order of five percent over the last 40 years.[42]

Encouraging citizen participation and expanding the voter base is a cherished Democratic Party ideal. In theory it's a good one— and an ideal shared by most Republicans. However, allegations that low voter registration and turnout in America is unrelated to what is happening in the rest of the world and caused instead by a concerted Republican effort to disenfranchise poor and minorities is stretching the truth and not substantiated by facts.

To seek to involve more Americans in the political process is a laudable activity. To seek to register just those that will bring votes to the Democratic (or Republican) is a legal but partisan activity. However, to use public funds to register just those that will bring in wanted voters and turn away or lose the registrations of those who might vote against you is illegal. It is also what ACORN was all about.

ACORN, the mother of all election fraud.
(The Association of Community Organizations for Reform Now) was founded in 1970 by Wade Rathke, who also founded Service Employees International Union (SEIU) Local 100, headquartered in New Orleans, which organizes public sector workers in Louisiana and Texas.[43] During the 1970s, ACORN was one of the first community organizers to take advantage of funding from the Community Reinvestment Act, which mandated banks to funnel capital investments into poor communities. Over the next thirty-plus years, ACORN developed significant skills at funneling publicly held bank and tax-payer dollars into its legally-separate political arm[44] . Involved in a well-publicized embezzlement scandal, with allegations of facilitating fraudulent registrations and other election fraud through the years, its activities in the first decade of the new millennium became too much even for Democrats in Congress. In September 2009, in a controversial but overwhelmingly bipartisan vote, Congress voted to defund ACORN and, under pressure, President Obama signed the bill later that year. But that didn't finish it. A district court judge initially struck down the law in December 2009, heralding a year of legal wrangling until the law finally was upheld when the US Supreme Court refused to hear an appeal to the Second Circuit US Court of Appeals reversal of the district court's decision.[45] On the 2 November

2010, ACORN filed for Chapter 7 bankruptcy.[46] However, ACORN may not be completely dead. In an article from December 11, Andrew Breitbart's online blog reported that despite reports made by HUD and GAO to the Affordable Housing Centers of America (AHCOA), an ACORN spinoff, received federal grants in contravention to the defunding act. This report came from an internal audit of Neighbor Works America (a quasi-government entity that includes HUD officials on its board), which has some of the federal funding responsibility for organizations like AHCOA and ACORN.[47] The Illinois Hardest Hit Program got a new director in early 2011, Joe McGavin, former director of counseling for ACORN Housing in Chicago and operations manager for Chicago ACORN offshoot, AHCOA (see the connection?). Soon after his appointment, Hardest Hit scored a $445 million grant of federal tax-payer dollars.[48] In Massachusetts, the New England United 4 Justice (NEU4J), another ACORN reincarnation run by Maude Hurd, formerly national president of ACORN, is suing the state for not registering enough low-income citizens during their trips to welfare offices. ACORN still exists, is still being funded by the Obama Administration. It has just been rebranded.[49]

The following is a list of particularly egregious ACORN registration and election fraud activities condensed from a table at RottenACORN.com.

The complete, detailed table may be found on their website.[50]

2009 Florida: 11 ACORN workers accused of forging voter registration applications in Miami-Dade County; statistical check revealed 197 of 260 did not match any living person.

Nevada: ACORN indicted on 26 counts of voter registration fraud and 13 counts of illegally compensating canvassers using bonus program called "Blackjack" or "21+" for canvassers registering more than 20 voters per shift.

Pennsylvania, Pittsburgh: 7 ACORN employees indicted for submitting falsified voter registration forms and 6 of 7 were indicted for registering voters under an illegal quota system.

2008 Connecticut: The New York Post reported ACORN submitted a voter registration card for a 7-year-old Bridgeton girl, 8,000 cards will be scrutinized for possible fraud.

Florida: Election officials in Brevard County have given prosecutors more than 23 suspect registrations from ACORN.

Florida: The state's Division of Elections is also investigating complaints in Orange and Broward Counties.

Indiana: Election officials threw out over 4,000 ACORN-submitted voter registrations after finding they had identical handwriting and dead voters.

Michigan: Detroit found numerous ACORN-submitted duplicate and fraudulent voter applications, which were turned over to the U.S. Attorney's office.

Missouri, Kansas City: 400 ACORN-submitted registrations rejected due to duplication or false information.

New Mexico: Prosecutors investigating more than 1,100 fraudulent ACORN-submitted voter registration cards, many with duplicate names and slightly altered personal information.

Nevada: State authorities raided ACORN's Las Vegas headquarters as part of a task force investigation of election fraud. Discovered fraudulent registrations included players from the Dallas Cowboys.

North Carolina: State Board of Elections investigating ACORN applications with similar or identical names, but with different addresses or dates of birth.

Ohio: According NY Post, ACORN activists gave residents cash and cigarettes in exchange for filling out voter registration cards. Some voters claimed to have registered dozens of times, and a man claimed to have signed 72 cards.

Pennsylvania: 57,435 voter registrations, most of them submitted by ACORN, thrown out by state election after clearly fraudulent signatures, vacant lot addresses, and fraud was detected.

Pennsylvania, West Reading: ACORN employee sentenced to 23 months in prison for identity theft and tampering with records.

Texas, Harris County: nearly 10,000 ACORN-submitted registrations were found to be invalid, many with clearly fraudulent addresses or personal information.

Texas: ACORN turned a voter registration with invented SSN and birth for already registered voter David Young, who told reporters "The signature is not my signature. It's not even close."

Wisconsin, Milwaukee: 2 charged with felonies when at least 33,000 ACORN-submitted registrations were called into question after it was found that felons were being used as registration workers.

2007 Missouri, Kansas City: 4 ACORN employees indicted for charges including identity theft and filing false registrations.

Ohio, Reynoldsburg: after being registered by ACORN to vote in two separate counties, man indicted on two felony counts of illegal voting and false registration.

Washington: 3 ACORN employees pleaded guilty, 4 more were charged with voter registration fraud for submitting over 2,000 fraudulent voter registration cards during a voter registration drive.

2006 Missouri, St. Louis: 8 ACORN employees indicted on federal election fraud charges for forging signatures and submitting false information.

2005 Colorado: Two ex-ACORN employees were convicted in Denver of perjury for submitting false voter registrations.

New Mexico, Albuquerque: 4 ACORN employees submitted as many as 3,000 potentially fraudulent signatures in ballot initiative. Local sheriff said forgery was widespread."

Virginia: An audit of Project Vote, an ACORN affiliate, revealed 83% of sampled registrations were rejected for false or questionable information, other people's SSN, non-existent or commercial addresses, or convicted felons

Virginia: State Board of Elections warned ACORN that 56% of registration applications and 35% were not submitted in a timely manner. The letter went on to state that there appeared to be evidence of intentional vote fraud and that information appeared to have been altered on some applications where information given by the applicant in one color ink was been scratched through and re-entered in another color ink.

2004 Colorado: An ACORN employee admitted to forging signatures and registering three of her friends to vote 40 times.

Michigan: The Detroit Free Press reported ACORN-affiliate Project Vote was one of two groups suspected of attempting to register nonexistent people or forging applications for already-registered voters

Minnesota: Police found over 300 voter registration cards in the trunk of a former ACORN employee, violating legal requirements.

New Mexico: An ACORN employee registered a 13-year-old boy to vote; accused by State Rep. Joe Thompson for "manufacturing voters" throughout New Mexico.

North Carolina: Officials investigated ACORN for submitting fake voter registration cards.

Ohio, Cuyahoga County: ACORN and affiliate Project Vote submitted registration cards with the highest errors rate of any voter registration group.

Ohio, Columbus: ACORN employee indicted for submitting a false signature and false voter registration form.

Ohio, Franklin County: two ACORN employees submitted what the director of the board of election supervisors called "blatantly false" forms.

Pennsylvania, Berks County: Director of Elections stated that vote fraud was absolutely out of hand and that there were both unintentional and blatant intentional duplicate voter registrations. Deputy Director added that ACORN was under investigation by the Department of Justice.

Pennsylvania, Reading: Director of Elections received numerous complaints that ACORN employees deliberately put inaccurate information on their voter registration forms.

Wisconsin: District attorney's office investigated 7 voter registration applications filed by Project Vote employees in the names of people who said the group never contacted them. Former Project Vote employee Robert Marquise Blakely told the Milwaukee Journal Sentinel that he had not met with any of the people whose voter registration applications he signed.

2003 Missouri, St. Louis: only 2,013 of 5,379 ACORN-submitted voter registration cards appeared to be valid. At least 1,000 are believed to be attempts to register voters illegally.

1998 Arkansas: A contractor with ACORN-affiliated Project Vote was arrested for falsifying about 400 voter registration cards.

7. Election fraud—case after case

*Those on all sides of this debate have
acknowledged that in-person voting fraud is
uncommon.—Eric Holder, US Attorney General*[51]

Really, General Holder? In an earlier chapter, we laid out example after example of bad registrations as an enabler of election fraud. In this chapter we present example after example of election fraud, consistently used over the decades, consistent with the Democratic Party philosophy that the people are too stupid or uninformed to support all the government they need, so elections must be won by any means possible.

In the words of Speaker Nancy Pelosi, "We have to pass the bill so you can find out what is in it."[52] The implication: Americans cannot be trusted to support legislation in their own interest; neither can they be trusted to elect the right sort of people. So resorting to election fraud is necessary and moral in the pursuit of the betterment of the very people, who vote against them. This is all nonsense of course, and our description would be denied by Democrats. However, the actions of the Democrat political class clearly demonstrate that it is part of their belief system.

Wisconsin District 21 Senate Recall 2012

As is the case in most close elections and recounts, just a few fraudulently cast votes could make the difference. However, vote fraud is a hard to prove crime. Winners don't usually pursue it and losers don't usually have the resources or the force of government to ensure that it is pursued. Unless the vote is within state guidelines for a recount, nothing usually happens. Statutes of limitations are short and people lose interest as the election fades. Just as with crimes of espionage, unless a poll worker is caught red handed fiddling with the count or voting an unused registration, at the end of the day that kind of fraud just isn't easily detectable. So it was Wisconsin State Senate recall between Republican State Senator Van Wanggaard and Democrat John Lehman. In a very dirty election with protests and threatened lawsuits from petition to conclusion, thousands of out of state union members bussed in on Election Day, lost and found ballots on Election Day, and petitions for recounts, John Lehman found himself ahead by 834 votes on 15 June, 10 days after the primary. This was a significant election, WI Governor Scott Walker and several Republican Senators had kept their seats in the recall—but this election would change control of the Senate. Petitions followed and a recount was conducted, reducing Lehman's lead to 819 by 2 July. Ultimately, Wanggaard decided not to contest the election but concentrate on his campaign to retake his seat.[53] The general election is in Nov 2012 and it is unlikely that the Governor will call the part-time legislature into session until a long term majority is decided in November. Was there fraud involved or was it just close? Many suspicions existed and the legitimacy of the election was brought into question. With clean voter rolls and Voter ID, none of this would have happened and whoever the winner might have been, as well as the voters, would have been assured a legitimate outcome.

Rangel-Espaillat Primary 2012 In New York City, the Democratic Party machine does not only target Republicans. New York State Senator Andriano Espaillat was confident when he challenged 21 term Congressman Charlie Rangel in the 24 June primary. After all, redistricting had added much of Espaillat's Senate constituency into the 13th congressional district and Rangel was still in disgrace after being censured by the House Ethics Committee. But the party establishment wanted Rangel. On Election Day, Rangel lead by 807 votes and an additional 2,600 paper ballots counted on Thursday increased that lead by another 131. However, the election board had thrown out 2,000 paper ballots from Espaillat's neighborhood as invalid and accusations flew that voters with Dominican accents had been turned away at the polls being told they were not eligible.[54] By early July, suits were filed. But in the end, Espaillat, facing a deadline to file to keep his State Senate seat, dropped everything and the Democratic Party will use this primary as an example that no one was convicted of vote fraud and no voter suppression was confirmed (only Republicans do that, they say). Rangel, the censured Congressman with decades of questionable ethics, will likely keep his seat in November and again take an oath to "preserve, protect, and defend the Constitution" when he takes his seat in Congress for the 22nd time in January 2013.

Wisconsin Supreme Court. During an April 2011 election for Wisconsin, a critical race for the Supreme Court and vital to Gov. Scott Walker's budget reform efforts, the race was expected to be very close. After the count, the conservative candidate, David Prosser, was found to be behind by 204 votes. Only then did the Waukesha County Clerk Kathy Nickolaus find an additional 14,315 ballots from Brookfield, a Republican stronghold expected to support Prosser. These votes added an additional 7,582 to Prosser, giving him a 7,316 lead.[55] The official explanation was that the tally was lost in a computer, and that the error stemmed from incompetence rather than conspiracy, but the loser, Joanne Kloppenburg, demanded and received a recount at the cost of a half million dollars to the taxpayer; Prosser's victory was upheld with a margin of 7,006.[56] The perception of fraud is widespread in Wisconsin, and both parties have been guilty. However, the editorials at the time on both sides were convinced that fraud had been committed. The rancor over this election foreshadowed the recall battle in 2012, where allegations, fraud, and certainly voter intimidation were commonplace.

2009 local vote fraud. In Troy NY, four local officials and Democratic Party activists were convicted in 2011 for forging enough absentee ballots to change the outcome of city council and county elections. Two of the operatives claimed that fraud was a normal way of insuring election victory. One of those convicted, Anthony DeFiglio was quoted as saying that vote fraud was a "normal political tactic" and that the targets were low income housing residents, because they didn't ask a lot of questions. [57]

Virginia 2008 vote fraud. In April 2012, an investigation stemming from the 2008 general election had convicted 38 people out of 400 submitted by the Virginia state police stemming from an investigation of the election. Some of the remaining cases are still outstanding. Donald Palmer, secretary of the Virginia Board of Elections stated that "We believe these complaints ran the gamut from voter registration fraud issues through potential fraud at the polling place on Election Day," He went on to say that the results of the state police investigation "remind us that unfortunately, fraud does exist in Virginia's elections." Of the original 400 cases to be investigated, 194 cases where a violation had been determined were dropped for various reasons including incorrect names, inability to locate individuals, and statement by the individuals that they believed they were entitled to vote. Ten indictments were against felons, who had lied on their registration forms.[58]

Minnesota convicts fraudulent voters from 2008. On 13 Oct 2011, the state convicted 113 ineligible voters, who knowingly voted illegally and over 200 cases still remained outstanding. This was the largest wholesale conviction since 1936, when 259 fraudulent voters were convicted in Jackson County, Missouri. The president of a Minnesota voter organization, Minnesota Majority, discussed the difficulty of convicting fraudulent voters, "These convictions are just the tip of the iceberg, the actual number of illegal votes cast was in the thousands. Most unlawful voters were never charged with a crime because they simply pled ignorance. We have evidence of these people casting illegal ballots, but in Minnesota, ignorance of election law is considered to be an acceptable defense." Davis went to say, "The problem rests largely on our current Election Day registration system. Most of the fraudulent votes cast in 2008 could have been prevented by using the normal registration and verification processes. But since the Election Day registration process does not include eligibility verifications, it simply leaves the door open to these kinds of abuses." [59]

Milwaukee 2004 election fraud. Like St. Louis and Chicago, Milwaukee has a long reputation for vote fraud. However, it has an additional fraud-enabler, same day registration. In Feb 2008 the Milwaukee Police Department Special Investigations unit released a report on an investigation of the 2004 presidential election, which had been decided by fewer than 12,000 votes. That report found ballots cast by ineligible voters, over 220 felons voted, felons were employed as poll workers, out of state college students voted in Wisconsin, individuals cast multiple votes, and out of state Kerry campaign workers voted in Wisconsin illegally. Besides the fraudulent activity, gross incompetence was found in the election commission office, including: 4,600 to 5,300 more ballots cast than voters signing in; and over 1,300 same-day registration cards indecipherable or invalid. At nearby Marquette University that year, a little over 2,600 people lived on campus but 5,217 voters were registered in one dorm, Sandberg Hall—little doubt of registration fraud there. No prosecutions were filed because the incompetence of the election officials and slovenliness of election documents was so universal it left prosecutors with little solid chain of evidence[60] To the Democrats no conviction means no election fraud, and even a conviction is discounted. Yet fraud was highly likely and the perception of fraud continues to damage the legitimacy of the US voting system.

8. Suppressing whose vote?

So here we are, just two months away from the election, with more and more examples that modern day Jim Crow laws are alive and well in the state of Florida.—Corrine Brown[61], US Representative (D-FL)

Democrats like Representative Corrine Brown claim that Voter ID is an evil plot by the Republicans to suppress the vote but this is not even close to true. While there are certainly stories of local Republicans making it hard for people to vote, establishment Democrats have used every means from disenfranchising voters from Jim Crow to supporters of Jimmy Carter. Democrats have shown, with distressing regularity, a willingness to throw every roadblock they can find to suppress either the voting or the counting of the voting, before or after the election, of citizens that might cast their ballot for the other candidate.

Jim Crow laws and African American disenfranchisement: The colloquially named Jim Crow laws are local and state laws dating from the period of Reconstruction until Federal legislation and Supreme Court action in the mid-1960s. As regards voting rights, such pernicious laws as the poll tax, and literacy tests, were finally put to rest by the Voting Rights act of

1965. Although Democrats attempt to blame Republicans for most everything discriminatory, it is illuminating to note that these discriminatory laws were the doing of white southern Democrats, beginning with their return to power in the South at the end of Reconstruction with the acquiescence of Northern Democrats, who desired their political support nationally.

In fact the election of Woodrow Wilson, the first Southern-born President since the Civil war, was greatly aided by the exclusion of southern African Americans from the vote—and he quickly returned the favor by implementing segregation in federal offices. Democrats born during the Civil War built solid southern Democratic Party majorities, and, to maintain them, they legislated discriminatory state laws, including voting limitations, segregation, and other limitations of the legal rights of African Americans.

The Jim Crow laws the Democrats often like to point to was a Southern problem, not a Republican one. And some southern Democrats resisted the repeal of those laws. While the votes in Congress for the 1965 Voting Rights Act were solidly bipartisan, they were overwhelmingly Republican, with some southern resistance within the Democratic Party ranks. Nearly half a century later both parties have passed beyond such things but the Democrats would like to twist the facts through blurring the memory of history and connect Republicans rather than themselves to old evils. This is easy to do, of course. Americans are particularly ignorant of anything that happened more than a decade or so ago. In fact in a poll taken in the mid-1990s, about 70 of juniors in Texas high schools thought the US was allied to the Germans fighting the Russians in WWII (for you that are historically challenged, it was the other way around).

New Black Panther Prosecution. Based on alleged voter intimidation activities in 2008, the Bush Department of Justice initiated an investigation of the New Black Panther Party later in that year. Soon after taking office, the Obama Department of Justice quietly dropped the case. For several years, the administration claimed that the case was dropped for lack of evidence and that no political leadership had been involved in the decision. Judicial Watch, having been denied documents requested under the Freedom of Information Act (FOIA) eventually sued and was able subsequently to secure many unavailable documents. Later Judicial Watch sued for attorney's fees and, not surprisingly, Obama Department of Justice claimed that none were due since "none of the records produced in this litigation evidenced any political interference whatsoever in" the New Black Panther Party case.

In July 2012, US District Court Judge Reggie Walton sided with Judicial Watch, writing, "The documents reveal that political appointees within DOJ were conferring about the status and resolution of the New Black Panther Party case in the days preceding the DOJ's dismissal of claims in that case, which would appear to contradict Assistant Attorney General Perez's testimony that political leadership was not involved in that decision. Surely the public has an interest in documents that cast doubt on the accuracy of government officials' representations regarding the possible politicization of agency decision-making."[62] Democrats practicing voter intimidation—never! Couldn't happen. Remember Democrats claim that only nasty Republicans do this to intimidate African Americans, Hispanics, and poor people. Here it was used in the primaries to intimidate Hillary Clinton voters, and in the general to intimidate Bush Voters. While neither party has a spotless history, it is clear, at least for voter intimidation, that Democrats are willing to accuse their opponents for doing what they themselves do.

Overseas voter disenfranchisement—citizen intent questionnaire. For the upcoming 2012 election, the Federal Government added a question on the Federal Write-in Absentee Ballot (FWAP) that caused considerable concern among overseas residents. It added a question asking if the citizen abroad intended to return. Concern that a yes question might trigger additional federal tax and that a no answer might cause loss of citizenship, the question was seen as causing potential disenfranchisement. A firestorm arose among the expatriate community and the government was forced to allow the old forms to be used and assured voters in the FAQ at fvap.gov as follows:

"Can my selection in Block 1 of the Federal Post Card Application or Federal Write-in Absentee Ballot affect my U.S. citizenship?

"No. The U.S. Department of State confirms that residing abroad with no intent to return to a particular state or to any state is not a potentially expatriating act that could result in loss of U.S. citizenship. Checking "I do not intend to return" will not result in loss of your U.S. citizenship. Persons who wish to renounce U.S. citizenship abroad must take an oath of renunciation before a U.S. diplomatic or consular officer at a U.S. embassy or consulate abroad."[63]

9. Voting and our troops

We sleep safely at night because rough men stand ready to visit violence on those who would harm us.—Winston Churchill[64], British Prime Minister, WWII

As we enter the 2012 election cycle, our deployed military and overseas citizens have a far better chance to have their votes counted than in years previous. At the very least new requirements for states and counties to provide timely ballots and new procedures are being implemented by the Federal Voter Assistance Program (FVAP, which) should reduce the primary reason military overseas voters have been disenfranchised—ballots sent so late they cannot be returned in time to count.

Credit this to the 2002 Help America Vote Act (HAVA) and the Military Overseas Voter Empowerment (MOVE) Act signed into law in 2009. Too late to be completely implemented for the 2010 elections, in 2012 this law provides a one stop website for the military overseas voter, FVAP.gov, and requires the Department of Justice to sue states our counties that mail ballots late (less than 45 days before the election. Unfortunately, the Department of Justice has to date not complied with the legal requirement to hold election commissioners accountable, at least not if they're Democrat; and MOVE is silent on the types of efforts exerted by the Democrats in 1996 and 2000 to have military absentee ballots declared invalid.

The challenges faced by our deployed military as they try to vote is nothing new, nor are the roadblocks erected by the Democrats. The mid-term election of 1862 was the first US election where voting rights of the US military (at that time soldiers, sailors, and marines) was a significant issue. Before that the US had only a small standing Army and Navy. By the end of 1862, the Union Army had grown to 521,204 and to over one million by the presidential election in 1864. In September of that year, President Abraham Lincoln wrote to General William T. Sherman, requesting he permit Indiana soldiers to return home for a state election. Most northern states made accommodations for soldiers to vote, usually by proxy or by sending election commissioners to their state regiments. Wisconsin was the first state to legalize absentee voting in 1862. Democrats, fearful that soldiers would vote Republican to support both abolition and the Commander in Chief, made efforts to disenfranchise soldiers wherever possible. In fact only about 150 thousand of the one million troops voted. And the Democrats were right, 119,754 voted for Lincoln and only 34,291 voted for George McClellan[65], the bitter Democratic former General that Lincoln had relieved after his failures in the Peninsula Campaign and at Antietam.[66]

Union veterans became more politically active than ever before in the nation's history after the Civil War. Founded in Decatur, IL, on 6 April 1866 by Benjamin F. Stephenson, the Grand Army of the Republic (GAR) was an association of Civil War veterans of the Union Army, Navy, Marine Corps, and Revenue Cutter Service (now Coast Guard). Organized around posts, much like the modern VFW, the GAR began as a fraternal organization but evolved into a significant political one, with membership of 409,489 by 1890.[67] Continuing further to cement the relationship between the armed forces of the Union with the Republican Party, the GAR, first supported Union soldiers running for political office and later supported pensions for war widows and orphans. While the GAR was extremely influential within 19th century Republican Party, such an affiliation was less clear among active military, where officers supported their members of Congress or governors in return for patronage and enlisted were essentially apolitical.[68]

After the Civil War, with the exception of short term increases in size during the Spanish American War and WWI, after which forces rapidly returned to a small size, the military was a small professional force, generally apolitical. During WWI the United States participation in Europe lasted only three years and U.S. forces were only absent during one mid-term election[69] During the 1930s, typically less than 30 percent of officers voted, and many, including General George C. Marshall, expressed concerns whether it was even ethical for a military officer to vote for his Commander and Chief. Believing that military officers should distance themselves from politics, General Eisenhower is not believed to have voted until after leaving active service.[70]

During WWII, military officer voting remained low and enlisted even lower. By 1940 most states required registration, with 18 of them requiring registration in person; several states had constitutional barriers to absentee voting. Most southern states required a poll tax, although Mississippi and South Carolina exempted military personnel. Despite Department of War instructions to aid and encourage soldiers to vote, it remained very difficult to do so; during the 1942 mid-term election only a half percent of the over five million active service members cast their vote. The first national military voting rights bill was introduced by Rep. Donald Ramsay (D-WV) in 1942. Although initially opposed by the War Department and National Association of Secretaries of State, changes were made to the bill and it was passed and signed into law on

September 16, 1942, with some opposition by southern Democratic members of Congress on state's rights issues and because the bill eliminated poll taxes for military members. The law specified that a postcard be provided to each military voter to request a ballot via their home state's Secretary of State. A ballot, with only federal offices was included. Upon swearing an oath in front of an officer that the member was a qualified voter in the state and witnessed by the officer, the ballot was mailed back.[71]

In 1944, Democrats seeing an opportunity in votes from large conscript military population, pressed for amendments to include requests to the States to make it easier for all soldiers and sailors to vote and the inclusion of a limited federal ballot. Republicans, believing that fewer military would provide advantage, opposed the bill, but it passed and signed into the law on 1 April 1944, just in time for the upcoming election. Of the 9.2 million on active duty at the time, 4.4 requested ballots, and 2.6 million of voting aged (then 21) military returned them for a 29.1 percent turnout, compared to 60 percent of eligible civilians. Military absentee voting accounted for about 5.6 percent of the total popular vote for president.[72]

In 1948 and 1950 overseas election data was not collected but military turnout was believed to have declined. In 1951 President Harry S.

Truman requested the American Political Science Association to examine military voting and make recommendations.[73] In receipt of that study in 1952 President Truman wrote a letter to Congress encouraging passage of the measure,

"About 2,500,000 men and women in the Armed Forces are of voting age at the present time. Many of those in uniform are serving overseas, or in parts of the country distant from their homes. They are unable to return to their States either to register or to vote. Yet these men and women, who are serving their country and in many cases risking their lives, deserve above all others to exercise the right to vote in this election year. At a time when these young people are defending our country and its free institutions, the least we at home can do is to make sure that they are able to enjoy the rights they are being asked to fight to preserve."[74]

In that letter, Truman went on to request Congress to pass a temporary law based on the recommendations to ensure that a better overseas voting process was implemented prior to the mid-term elections in 1954. It did not happen. The Korean War ended in 1952, the troops came home, and the issue moved to the back burner. It was not until much later that Congress passed the bill that established the basis for the overseas military voters programs we have today. President Dwight Eisenhower signed the Federal Voting

Assistance Act into law in 1955.[75] The act created the Federal Voting Assistance Program (FVAP), which greatly modified, still exists today. FVAP, which assists both military and civilian overseas voters, is managed out of the Department of Defense. Tasked since 1956 with reporting to the President and Congress after each Federal election, archived reports of elections since 1962 are available at the FVAP.gov website at (www.fvap.gov/reference/pesurveyrpts.html).76

Based on 20 years' experience with the FVAP, including the Viet Nam War, Congress passed a replacement and updated law, the Overseas Citizens Voting Rights Act. This act has been further updated and enhanced three times since then: Uniformed and Overseas Citizens Absentee Voting Act (UOCAVA) in 1986; Help America Vote Act (HAVA) in 2002[77], which included reforms based on experience gained during the 2000 presidential election; and the Military and Overseas Voter Empowerment Act (MOVE) in 2009[78], which, among other things, mandated states to send ballots to overseas military voters at least 45 days in advance of an election and significantly increased funding resources for the FVAP.

The highlighted findings from the 2008 Post Election Survey Report are summarized here:[79]

"In October 2009, UOCAVA was amended by the Military and Overseas Voter Empowerment Act (MOVE Act) which was enacted as part of the FY 2010 National Defense Authorization Act (P.L. 111-84). The MOVE Act: requires that absentee ballots be sent at least 45 days in advance; requires States make blank ballots and voter registration and absentee ballot application information available electronically; expands the use of the Federal Write-in Absentee Ballot; and removes outdated notarization requirements."

"Active duty military vote at greater rates than the national population (when adjusted for age and gender differences), and are registered to vote at rates greater than the national electorate, even before adjusting for age and gender differences.

"Specific findings of this survey include: 77% of active duty military were registered to vote for the 2008 general election while 86% of Federal employees living overseas were registered to vote. By comparison, only 71% of the U.S. Census CVAP [Civilian Voting Age Population-ed.] was registered to vote. When adjusted to match the demographic composition of the U.S. Census national CVAP, the active duty military registration rate in the 2008 general election was 87%. 54% of active duty military members and 76% of Federal employees living overseas voted in the 2008 general election. 63.6% of the national

CVAP voted in the 2008 general election. When adjusted to match the demographic composition of the national CVAP, the active duty military voting participation rate in the 2008 general election was 73%."

Now this all sounds very good. Military is registered higher than the general population and more of them vote. But look at the statistics surrounding return and voting failure rates.

"The overall UOCAVA voter absentee ballot return rate was 67%, whereas the non-UOCAVA domestic national absentee ballot return rate was 91%.

"The absentee ballot return rate for active duty military in the U.S. was 63%. The absentee ballot return rate for active duty military overseas was 67%. 17% of registered active duty military said they requested an absentee ballot but did not receive it.

"The absentee ballot return rate for overseas civilians was 74%. 94% of returned UOCAVA voter ballots cast were counted.

"**The majority of voting failure is in ballot transmission and return** [emphasis mine]:

"For all UOCAVA voters, 1.4% of the voting failure they experienced was in registration or absentee ballot application failures with another

7.0% in ballot delivery failure, **78.2% in ballots transmitted but not returned** [emphasis mine], and 13.4% in ballots cast but not counted.

"For military voters, the rates were similar, with 1.5% of the voting failure in registration and absentee ballot application failures with another 7.5% in ballot delivery failure, **77.6% in ballot transmitted but not returned** [emphasis mine], and 13.4% in ballots cast but not counted.

"For overseas civilian voters, 0.6% of their voting failure was during registration or absentee balloting process, 85% in combined ballot delivery and return failure and 14.4% in ballots cast but not counted. The ballot delivery failure for overseas civilian voters was not separately determinable from the survey responses provided by Local Election Officials, and therefore is assumed to be in the ballots transmitted but not returned failures."

The report concluded with four issues/recommendations: voters need to get ballots at least 60 days ahead of time; postal delays exacerbate late ballot delivery; state by state absentee ballot requirements are too complex and different; and the new FVAP.gov website has substantially improved the absentee voting process but is not well publicized. The first recommendation is the most significant and is quoted in full bellow:

"**UOCAVA voters need their absentee ballots sent to them at least 60 days before they are due back to the election officials**. [emphasis mine] Military and overseas civilian voters are systematically denied an equal opportunity to vote by absentee ballot systems which rely exclusively on postal mail delivery, and which do not send out ballots early enough to be received, voted, and returned in time to meet absentee ballot deadlines. As reports such as the Pew Center on the States' No Time to Vote study detail, the absentee voting process often takes longer than individual States and territories provide their voters, who often see the process as unnecessarily cumbersome. To remedy this, more time must be provided for postal mail delivery to make the round-trip from Local Election Official (LEO) to voter and back to LEO, and greater use of electronic blank ballot delivery, such as email and online posting or transmission, needs to be offered by each State to overcome these unique obstacles."

Note the bold conclusion of the agency report, "**Military and overseas civilian voters are systematically denied an equal opportunity to vote...**"[emphasis mine] In its own interpretation of the numbers, the Military Voter Protection Project estimated that only about 20 percent of the 2.5 million overseas military voters were able to request and return their absentee ballots. With the failure rates presented above it is possible that only 5.1 percent had their votes counted.

The 2010 Post Election Survey Report[80] presented several encouraging trends: military participation rates rose over the comparison election, 2006 and the military voter registration rate remained high, 85 percent, in a non-presidential election year, dropping less than the CVAP at large. More states provided voter assistance tools to UOCAVA voters, both military and civilian voters, and many states enacted improved legislation to ease military and overseas voting. FVAP was provided more resources for communications and outreach, including a new one-stop website for ease of registration and ballot request.

Again, this dry Department of Defense report sounds very good. But the report goes on to say **"Unfortunately, 29% of active duty military voters indicated they never received the absentee ballot they requested, up from 16% in 2008. That represents approximately 120,000 active duty military personnel who never received their absentee ballot."** [emphasis mine] It is significant to note here that this is a larger number than the margin of victory in the 1960 Kennedy/Nixon election and when combined with the number of ballots that arrived too late to be counted, it is on the order the margin of victory for several other modern presidential races. According to the MVP Project effective turnout, or number of votes actually counted, for 2010 was even lower than 2008, 4.6 percent, since it was a mid-term election.

Improvements in overseas voter registration 2012 vs. 2008. During the 2008 election, in reaction to HAVA, the states began significant changes to rules regarding overseas registration and voting. Rules differed for military and non-military overseas voters and varied significantly between states. Faxed registrations were allowed by 28 states and DC and 7 more allowed e-mailed registrations as well. However, most required follow-up mailed registrations and some only allowed use of fax or email if active military with overseas duty. One state, Utah, restricted its use to a hostile fire zone—and then required a mailed follow-up. More states and DC, 42, allowed ballot requests by fax, with an additional 5 allowing e-mail as well. However, 34 states and DC required snail mail follow-up. Several only allowed the requests from military voters, and one, Missouri, had different rules for different counties. Faxed ballots were allowed by 39 with 16 allowing e-mail as well. However, numerous states restricted this to military in certain emergency situations such as later receipt of ballots and one state, Illinois, only allowed it for the Democrat strongholds of Chicago and Cook County.[81]

This author was serving in Afghanistan during the 2008 election and domiciled in Queens County, Maryland. Although Maryland at that time did not allow electronic transmission of materials from the war zone, the Queen Anne's County Registrar responded personally to my e-mailed request for registration materials with .pdf documents for me to fill in and mail back. Upon receipt the registrar sent me an email acknowledging receipt of the documents. Both registration and ballot request were allowed to be submitted together and my ballot was sent to me in a timely manner. This was not the case for most military and overseas voters in 2008, according to the Military Voter Protection Project only 5.6% of whom had ballots returned in time to be counted.[82]

For 2012, voter registration and ballot requests should be much easier. Based on the implementation of new requirements set out in the MOVE act of 2009, the FVAP has implemented a one-stop website, fvap.gov, which provides registration and ballot request materials online. For all states and territories, a voter can fill out the either the Federal Post Card Application or a state form and return either electronically or by mail as required by the individual state.[83] Thirty two states and DC now allow military and overseas voters to return their ballots by fax, e-mail, or web portal, while 3 allow electronically transmitted blank ballots to be returned by mail. Although this will increase the ease of overseas voting, there is increasing concern with the security of such voting and most states view 2012 as a pilot year.[84]

10. Soldier, you don't deserve to vote!

Our friend also mentioned the soldier vote, which we have all been hearing so much about lately. If that isn't the rawest political joke and farce I've ever heard of! I just have to laugh. Sure they want us to vote. Like heck they do. Someone back there is afraid we will all vote for the wrong man.—RT2 CL Maschinot, USS Salt Lake City, 1944[85]

Democrats object to activities such as Voter ID, purging voter rolls of aliens and felons, and deleting old, multiple registrations of citizens that have moved and re-registered in another place. The argument used by Democrats is that this might disenfranchise some hapless voter in some unusual circumstance. Despite court decisions, academic studies, and bipartisan commissions that dispute this, disenfranchisement is the major argument made by Democrats against cleaning things up or requiring proof that a voter is the person requesting the ballot.

But there really is disenfranchisement. It is an old problem and, believe it or not, it is not getting better over time—especially in counties and states controlled by Democrats. The votes of our military personnel serving overseas are not getting counted. And some of the Democratic Party intelligentsia even justify it!

To understand the moral justification made by these Democratic Party elite to disenfranchise the military, it is useful to see the perspective revealed in an academic paper entitled, "The Bullying of America: A cautionary tale about civil-military relations and voting reform" by University of Florida Law Professor, Diane H. Mazur. She begins by claiming a veteran's perspective (short-term peacetime service in the USAF 1979-1983) and then goes on to write, "The state of our civil-military relations and the health of our civilian control of the military are, simply, not good. This country missed a barrage of warning signals sent from Florida during November 2000 that should have alerted us to the need for open discussion of the constitutional, political, and cultural status of the military within American society." She then continues to denigrate our military by writing, "The shift to an all-volunteer force transformed the military into an institution that was less ideologically representative of larger society and less respectful of its constitutional obligation of political neutrality ... and has also weakened the professional military ethic of subordination to civilian authority, the central ethic underlying civilian control of the military."

She continues to go on, most shockingly, to accuse, "the military's conduct at Abu Ghraib was facilitated by an unspoken mindset within the military and its civilian leadership that they alone have the discretion to make decisions on the basis of perceived military necessity, unconstrained by law or judicial review. This mindset has taken hold over the course of a generation of service members, abetted by the Court's success in shielding military policy from judicial review and by the increasingly self-selected nature of **an ideologically and politically partisan force** [emphasis mine]." [86]

Having established (in her own mind) that the military is "less respectful of its constitutional obligation of political neutrality" and that it is an "ideologically and politically partisan force" of Florida 2000 she claims "there were still more votes to be collected after Election Day, even after news of the undecided election had been broadcast around the world. No one knew how many votes might still arrive or for whom they might be cast (although Democrats and Republicans had their guesses), but without doubt they represented the only "new" votes to harvest, in contrast to those already cast on or before." Later in her paper, she implies that military members forgot their oath to "preserve, protect, and defend" the Constitution and sent in ballots after the close of the election—and, with that, concluded her justification for disenfranchisement against a "partisan force" without evidence other than fantastic speculation.

The Democratic Party elite have a long history of disliking or even hating our military. This author was a young sailor at the end of Viet Nam and still remembers being spat on and being called a baby killer by the protesters of the time. Those protesters have become the leadership of the Democratic Party today and again, they would turn our soldiers into monstrous, morally bankrupt killers "unconstrained by law." So no matter that our military be disenfranchised; not equal to other citizens, they should just shut up and do what they're told. To the Democratic Party intelligentsia, it is fair game to take whatever measures needed to keep a "partisan" military from exercising their constitutionally guaranteed right to vote.

An explanation of Democratic Party tactics in 2000 Florida? Certainly. A justification to disenfranchise the military in the future? Probably. Evidence shows that Attorney General Eric Holder and his Department of Justice seemed to be uncompelled by law or decency to require counties and states to end the delay of transmission of ballots to our overseas military voters in 2010 or the primaries of 2012. It is not a stretch to expect similar lack of action intended to prevent our service men and women from having their votes be counted in November 2012.

The 2001 example in Florida is perhaps the most systematic and disgraceful attempt by the

Democrats to disenfranchise overseas military voters in recent years. It was so bad that laws were passed in both 2002 (HAVA) and 2009 (MOVE), which specifically addressed, among other things, our troops' right to have their vote counted. The most recent law, the MOVE Act, will have direct bearing on the 2012 election.

The notoriety of the 2001 attempt to disenfranchise military voters stems from its blatancy in throwing out military votes already cast in the aftermath of an already lost election. However, overseas military voter disenfranchisement caused by delaying ballots until it is too late to return them by the election has been an historical tool commonly used at county and state levels. It goes like this: a state legislature enacts complex registration rules for overseas voters—such as notarization, witnessing, and certified mail requirements for registrations and ballots. Then materials are sent so late that military cannot comply in a timely fashion to get their ballots back in time. The MOVE Act addressed some of these issues for 2010 and 2012. However the States, mostly Democratic Party-controlled ones, are slow to comply.

Val Verde County, 1996. It was a bold prelude to the Democrat's attempt to steal the 2000 presidential election for Gore by stealing military votes in Florida. The Texas Rural Legal

Aid (TRLA) sought to overturn the election of two Republican candidates in 1996 by challenging the validity of military votes. The story goes like this: Republicans won the election if the 800 military absentee ballots were counted, but the Democrats won if they were excluded. Using federal funds through the Legal Services Corporation, the TRLA sued the county and the candidates in US District Court, claiming that the absent military should not be considered residents. With the approval of the Clinton-appointed Judge, Fred F. Biery, the TRLA sent out a 24-page deposition, which inquired into each voter's intentions about where they might live upon leaving the military.

Relying on the completed questionnaire, Judge Biery pointed to the answers of one voter, an Air Force Officer then stationed in Colorado. That officer had answered that he intended to return to Texas upon retirement but would likely settle in Austin or San Antonio, rather than Val Verde County. Based on this, the judge ruled that the Officer had no right to vote because his present intent was not to return to Val Verde County. In an absurd opinion, concurred with by the TRLA and the Texas Democratic Party, the Judge piously asserted that there was not a question of whether the officer had the right to vote but where. The two Democrats were awarded the election.[87] Effectively, of course, the opinion meant that the 800 military members subject to the decision were disenfranchised—domiciled, but unable to vote in Val Verde County, they were unable to vote anywhere.

It should be noted that it is of longstanding federal law and practice that a military member serving outside his home, selects a domicile. That domicile must have been where the military lived at the time he or she selected the domicile, usually either the place lived when entering the military or a duty station lived at during service and chosen to be the domicile until discharge. The military member pays taxes to the domicile, registers their vehicles there, and votes there—as opposed to the address they may be living while serving. But not in Val Verde Texas—there they pay their taxes, register their car, but, no, they cannot vote. The military members, whose right to vote were affected, were not even "made aware of the pendency of the suit, much less have they had the opportunity to present arguments as to why their ballots should be counted."[88]

Traditionally, the military and veteran vote leans Republican. In 2004, the veteran vote leaned 16 points to Bush over Kerry; even in 2008 veterans voted 10 points in McCain's favor over Obama.[89] The active military vote is harder to capture, but polls before the election in 2004 showed that military favored Bush over Kerry by a stunning 72 to 17 percent.[90] In any case, recent polling shows that active military favor

Republicans over Democrats about by about 60 to 40 percent. The right to have their vote counted will almost certainly be targeted again in November 2012.

Overseas military votes are regularly too late to count, "The problem has always existed, given the high degree of mobility of our fighting forces," said Eric Eversole, founder and executive director of the Military Voter Protection Project, a nonprofit organization based in Washington, D.C. But the issue is a bigger concern during a presidential election year with a military force totaling more than 3 million, including active-duty and reserve forces. In 2010, of the approximately 2 million military and overseas voters accounted for in data reported by the states to the Election Assistance Commission, only 4.6 percent of those voters were able to cast an absentee ballot that counted, according to the Military Voter Protection Project's analysis of that data from the federal Election Assistance Commission, which tracks participation in voting. The 2010 election number is 0.9 percent lower than the 5.5 percent of overseas military voters able to cast votes during the last comparable mid-term election in 2006, the organization concluded—a discouraging decline in view of the new laws intended to increase military participation.[91]

Obama administration prepares to disenfranchise military in 2012. Ohio attempted to accommodate overseas and returning troops by extending early voting for the military. The Obama Department of Justice sued, claiming that longer early voting for military was unconstitutional because it gave military different voting privileges than the general population at large. This despite the fact the federal laws, such as HAVA, make special accommodation for military because of duty overseas and many states have set up special absentee ballot application procedures for military, reflecting their special status. National Guard Association stated that it was offensive for the Obama campaign to suggest that it was arbitrary for military to get special consideration and the Romney campaign general counsel, Katie Bibber said, "'Last week, respected military groups intervened in the Obama campaign's lawsuit. They argue that it is absolutely constitutional to give military voters special flexibility in voting, and that it is offensive for the commander-in-chief's political campaign to argue otherwise. ... We agree with these military groups."[92]

11. Voting at sea, or not

The party of the man who wants to be the next commander in chief is trying to throw out the votes of the men and women he will be commanding.—Jim Post, Republican attorney, Duval County, Florida, 2000[93]

In service from 1976 until 2008, the USS Tarawa (LHA-1), amphibious assault ship, was one of the Navy's largest capital ships—only smaller than the giant carriers. At 820 feet long and displacing 38,900 tons, she had a Navy crew of over 960 officers and enlisted and carried an additional 2000-plus marines along with their 25 helicopters and a squadron of 8 Harrier AV-8B aircraft. During the presidential election of 2000, the Tarawa and her crew of nearly 3,000 voters were deployed in the Indian Ocean, off the coast of Yemen in response to the attack on the USS Cole on the 12th of October that year.

One of Tarawa's crew, LT John Russell, had voted for George Bush in the 2000 election. At approximately 0330 local time on the 18th of November he was awakened by the night duty officer. Concerned that this could be an emergency, he quickly dressed and hurried to his office, where he returned the call to his wife, Mary, who answered the phone to relay some disturbing news. She had just arrived home and had received a call from the elections office in Duval County, Florida. The woman on the phone had told her that her husband's absentee ballot had been disqualified. A few minutes later, she received another call from a Florida Republican Party representative telling her that her LT Russell's ballot was one of hundreds of other military overseas ballots protested by the Democrats. The Democrats were systematically checking overseas military ballots and protesting any without a postmark.

LT Russell had posted his ballot early to ensure a timely arrival. That ballot had not been postmarked by the ship's post office. Why? Because the ship's post office did not normally postmark mail—it was not required by regulation—and had only hand postmarked ballots mailed in the last few days before the election to ensure they would be counted if they were delayed in the mail. [94]

Matt Drudge's headline the next day was "Released: Democrat memo on how to disqualify military votes." Thinking it would streamline Democrat efforts to undo George Bush's victory by recount, a local lawyer hired to help the Democrat's efforts distributed a confidential memo, only intended for party officials, to county attorneys—one of whom was incensed and released it to the press.

All of this was caused by Mark Herron, a clever Democratic Party lawyer, who developed a blue print for rejecting overseas military votes. Herron listed 5 areas to focus: ensuring that the ballot had not been voted twice (reasonable); ensuring that signatures on registration and ballot matched (extremely subjective in practice); witness signature by a notary or witness over 18 years old (military does not have notaries while deployed and military regulations permit an officer signature to substitute); postmark (often neglected for free overseas mail by fleet post office procedure at the time); and detailed inspection of ballot request. With the exception of the first, these objections were intended to focus on trivial defects in a real voter's overseas ballot, not on substantial compliance as the law required. All in all, these requirements set a much higher bar for overseas military than for local voters. In the end, 1,527 postal ballots, many of them from deployed military, were rejected by county elections commissioners at the insistence of Democrat operatives using this picayune standard during the recount.

After several frustrating days of this nonsense, General Norman Schwarzkopf, criticized the Democratic Party efforts in Florida by saying, "It is a very sad day in our country when the men and women of the armed forces are serving abroad and facing danger on a daily basis

... and are denied the right to vote for the president of the United States, who will be their commander in chief."[95]

In the combative recount of the election, everything eventually wound up in the courts, of course. In upholding the military's right to vote the US District Court, N.D. Florida, Pensacola Division wrote in its ruling, "It is truly an unfortunate circumstance when a citizen of the United States is denied the fundamental right to vote, whether residing in one of the several States or residing overseas. It is even more unfortunate when a vote cast by a member of the Armed Forces serving abroad is rejected for no legitimate or compelling reason." The court went on to order, "Accordingly, the Court HEREBY ORDERS that any state statute, regulation, administrative rule, or procedure that rejects a federal write-in ballot, which has been signed pursuant to the oath provided therein, (A) solely because the ballot envelope does not have an APO, FPO, or foreign postmark; or (B) solely because there is no record of an application for a state absentee ballot; conflicts with federal law. It is further ORDERED that all federal write-in ballots rejected for the above stated reasons are declared valid."[96]

So egregious were the attempts of the Democrats to overturn the rights of overseas military to have their votes count, that several bills were considered in Congress at the time, ultimately resulting in HAVA (Help America Vote Act), signed into law Oct 29 2002,[97] which had the dual effect to make it easier for overseas military to cast votes and to amend the NVRA (Motor Voter) to require tighter election procedures and periodic scrubbing of registration rolls.

In the debates in the Senate over the new voting bill, Senator Wayne Allard (R, CO, 1997-2009) expressed the outrage felt by the American people at the disenfranchisement of overseas military. Here is part of his statement[98] made on the Senate floor to introduce his version, the Military Voter Support Act, parts of which were ultimately incorporated into HAVA: "The bad taste left in everyone's mouth after the Florida election debacle is certainly strongest in those who had their franchise questioned while, incredibly, they were away serving our country. Military men and women are forced to give up some opportunities during their military service that the rest of us can still enjoy. They surrender some of the freedom of speech, privacy and personnel liberty that we take for granted. But losing their right to vote is never something they agreed to face, and never something we should allow them to face."

Senator Allard went on to say, "I know that I was not the only one who felt outrage over this. My office received a flood of calls and letters from

Colorado citizens equally upset. I hope this bill proves to our uniformed voters that we not only value their service, we value their voice, and we value their right to vote."

Three of the key changes, which made it into HAVA, addressed specific efforts by Democrats to disenfranchise military in the past:

"The bill prohibits a state from disqualifying a ballot based upon lack of postmark or witness signature alone--this was the basis for most absentee ballot challenges in Florida. Technical faults beyond the control of the voter should not endanger their ballot."

"The bill secures the voting residence of a military voter as they travel on orders. It prevents a repeat of the 1997 Texas lawsuit challenging future intent of residency."

"It will allow polling places to be operated on military installations to serve military voters and others at the discretion of the appropriate service Secretary. The law against this was revived and enforced by the Clinton Administration for the 2000 elections."

Other points made dealt with the difficulties inherent in the uncertainties of military service:

"There is a Catch-22 for military voters who are discharged and move before an election but after the residency deadline. They cannot vote through the military absentee ballot system. Yet sometimes they are not able to fulfill deadlines to establish residency in a State. This bill allows them to use the proper discharge forms as a residency waiver and vote in person at their new polling site.

"Given the technologies available to us, it should be possible for the military to devise and run an efficient and reliable electronic voting program."

"After each election the Pentagon Federal Voting Assistance Program makes recommendations to each state on ways to improve the voting ability of absentee voters by state statute changes. This bill brings more attention to bear on these improvements--and hopefully generates more state legislature interest--by requiring the states to report on their implementation of these suggestions."

To summarize, Allard said, "I sincerely hope that military members understand that we in the Congress are as outraged as they are about the problems they experienced in voting." Congress agreed, and out of this debate, HAVA was eventually passed in 2002. In addition to making it easier for the military to vote, this bill set the groundwork for the currently hotly debated clean-up of voter rolls and implementation of Voter ID.

12. Stealing the whole enchilada

"We won the election, but they stole it from us."—
Richard Nixon[99], 37th President of the United States

Florida 2000. To put the 2000 Florida election and recount into perspective, we should remind ourselves that despite the numerous attempts to win the election through the courts, ballot manipulation, and multiple attempts to change the count through recounts—George Bush won the election. Despite the myths that the Democrats have tried to create after the fact, several academic studies and press reports show that had the recounts encompassed the whole state, rather than just a few counties, Bush's vote tally would have actually 8,000-10,000 higher than it ended up. In addition, had the Democratic Party and the press not been successful in spreading the falsehood that the polls had closed in the Florida Panhandle (on central time) nearly 8,000 additional votes would have been cast for Bush there as well. Bush won and the attempted theft of the 2000 election by fraud and shenanigans was revealed again as a Democratic Party tactic.

In his book, Stealing Elections, John Fund relates interviews he had with poll workers and at least two former law enforcement officers observing the polls in heavily Democratic precincts. It seems that significant things happened in the time between poll closing, when the election monitors had headed off for home, and the time the ballots got back to the election center for counting. Precinct officials were observed by these witnesses opening the ballot boxes. Now card punch ballots have the interesting attribute that there are no marks are made on the ballot, rather pre-perforated "chad" is pushed out of the ballot leaving a hole. It's fast and there is no real way to tell if the hole is punched at the polling place or afterward. The witnesses observed the poll workers taking handfuls of ballots and punching each one through the "Gore" hole; if the voter had already voted for Gore, then no change was made; but if the voter had voted for someone else, then two votes appeared (called an over vote) and the ballot could be challenged and thrown out. At least one witness followed the poll worker's car on the way to the election center via a lengthy, scenic route. All in all about 19,000 ballots were double punched in Democratic Palm Beach County. Did this happen anywhere else? Requests in summer of 2001 by statistician John Lott were ignored. We'll never know. However, analysis of the same Votamatic voting system in Harris County Texas showed only 0.7% over voted and in San Diego County California only 0.5% over votes. This compared with nearly 5 percent in Palm Beach; certainly something was going on. In fact the results of Palm Beach were stunning. Bush's lead was reduced 50,000 votes statewide to less than 1,500 after the Palm Beach ballots came in very late, around midnight. Did the Democrats wait until the polls were closed and the initial count was made and then do something about it?[100] We are not likely ever to know.

It has long been a Democratic Party claim that the 2000 election was stolen by George Bush in Florida. The myth has been perpetuated, along with the myth that there is no vote fraud, since 2000. Jesse Jackson, for one, still speaks of Florida as "the scene of the crime" where "[blacks] were disenfranchised. Our birthright stolen." Michael Moore created a fictional documentary, Fahrenheit 911.[101] Yet in two massive recounts conducted by two large news consortia, one headed by USA Today and the Miami Herald and the other by the New York Times, the results were quite different. From the USA Today findings released on May 11, 2001: George Bush would have won if Al Gore had gotten the manual recounts he requested in four counties; Bush would have won if the U.S. Supreme Court had not stopped the hand recount of under votes; Bush would have won using the two most widely used standards for recounting all disputed ballots, a recount never asked for by the Gore team, including over votes and Gore only would have won by the slimmest of margins (42-171 votes) using the two least used standards. The Palm Beach Post summed it up most succinctly, "Al Gore was doomed. He couldn't have caught George W. Bush even if his two best chances for an official recount had played out."[102]

Florida's polls closed at 7:00 PM in November 2000. For the Panhandle that meant 7:00 PM Central Standard Time, or an hour later than the rest of the state, which was on Eastern Standard Time. Voters in this part of the state, often called Florabama, are heavily Republican and military; Pensacola Naval Air Station is located in the western part of the Panhandle. In what many believe to be a Democratic Party disinformation campaign, aided and abetted by the national press, several national networks declared the polls to be closed an hour early for this area of Florida; CBS alone announced that the polls had closed in Florida 33 times between 7:00 PM Eastern and 7:00PM Central time. At 7:48 Eastern, the networks declared Gore winning Florida. In a poll conducted after the election, many Republican voters on their way or already in line to vote gave up upon hearing the news on TV or radio and just went home without voting at all. In a poll done later, John McLaughlin estimated that the misinformation dissuaded about 28,050 voters from voting, 64 percent of whom had planned to vote for Bush. In a similar study, Democratic operative Bob Beckel commissioned a study on the Panhandle voting, which gave Bush a hypothetical additional lead of about 8,000 votes. In another study conducted by the statistician John Lott for the academic journal, Public Choice, he studied turnout from 1976-2000 and concluded the early closing announcements may have cost Bush as many as 90,000 votes; using other analysis he projected a net loss of 7,500 to 10,000 votes.[103]

By nearly any standard, Bush won in Florida even though the Democrats pulled out all the stops from unsavory to blatantly fraudulent to make sure he didn't. It didn't work. However, by reducing the margin of his victory in Florida to a statistical tie and creating questions about the legitimacy of even that margin of victory, the Democratic Party's efforts succeeded in weakening the first term of Bush's presidency and creating a question of legitimacy, a myth they continue to spread today despite significant evidence to the contrary.

Missouri 2000. If it hadn't been for Florida, the election shenanigans in Missouri would have been big news. Rampant election fraud of almost every kind was tried by the Democrats in St. Louis, MO in the November 2000 election. Although well documented, this is just another myth to the Democrats; an excuse to disenfranchise poor and minority voters. In fact, the fraud in St. Louis was described by the left-leaning Brennan Center this way, "Even given allegations that were unsubstantiated, the rate of possible fraud remains low. The analysis below lays out the allegations, reasons to question each, and the facts that we now know."[104] The reality is that St. Louis City has a historic reputation for conducting some of the most corrupt elections in the country.

Writing about the comedy of errors in the St. Louis City election of 2000, local columnist Steve Hilton wrote a comic piece about dead, felons, and Ritzy the Dog all being registered voters. But it wasn't funny at all. Voting machines were abandoned, ballot boxes left unguarded, and when it was determined that the election was very close for the Governor and US Senate, the local circuit judge, Evelyn Baker, responding favorably to a suit filed by now Congressman Lacy Clay, who was running that year to inherit his father's seat. The suit was filed in the name of Bob Odam (later found to be dead), who was "concerned that he wouldn't be able to vote because of long lines..." The judge ordered the polls held open. Within minutes of that order, obviously pre-prepared robo-calls from Rev. Jesse Jackson began to go out into Democrat-heavy North Saint Louis informing them that the polls were being held open and, in what appeared to be coordinated action, KMOX and KDNL received phone calls from a pre-recorded Al Gore requesting stations encourage people to vote. In a race for time, The Missouri Court of Appeals overruled the circuit court, writing that the extended poll hours "would only permit voting by persons not entitled to participate." The Brennan Center called this game "allegations of irregularities unconnected to individual voter fraud." Later Mark Odam, Bob Odams' son and an operative of Bill Clay, claimed that it was a misunderstanding and that he was named to testify not his father. However, it was later found that Mark Odam had voted earlier in the day and had no need to hold the polls open—unless, perhaps, it was to vote a second time as his father. To the Democrats this was "unconnected to individual voter fraud," of course. Move on; nothing to see here!

In the aftermath of the election confusion, election judges at 29 of 400 precincts walked away from their poll assignments leaving ballot boxes in care of building custodians. The next day an abandoned voting machine was found in a vacant lot. Later in an investigation by the Missouri Secretary of state, Matt Blunt, found 56,000 duplicate registrations in the St. Louis area alone.

Nearly 54,000 voters out of a total 125,230 had been designated as "inactive" and had to confirm their registration at the election board downtown. The election judges, all of them

Democrats, issued nearly five hundred orders allowing people to vote without allowing any challenge by present Republican observers. Voters were given orders to be allowed to vote without any evidence of prior eligibility or registration, with acceptable reasons ranging from "For the Democratic Party" to "I...was a felon...I didn't know that I had to register again to vote." In his investigation, Matt Blunt found that only 35 of 1,286 court orders met the legal standard required by Missouri Law. In his report he noted that in the city of St. Louis, NVRA (Motor Voter) had facilitated fraud. The city had an impossibly high 96 percent registration rate; 62 federal and 52 state felons voted illegally; 68 people voted twice; 79 people registered in vacant lots; 14 dead voted; and 45 election judges were not even registered to vote themselves, as required. In addition he cited 250 non-residential addresses, over a quarter of which were likely drop-sites used for false voter registrations, based on random sampling.[105]

The results of the election were astounding but maybe not surprising. Dead Democratic Governor Mel Carnahan beat incumbent US Senator John Ashcroft by 49,000 votes and Carnahan's successor, Bob Holden, appointed Carnahan's widow to the job; then US Representative Jim Talent lost an even closer battle with Bob Holden for Governor by 10,000 votes.[106] Did fraud make the difference? The Brennan Center says no but US Senator Kit Bond (R-MO) said of the election, "I think the evidence points very strongly to a major criminal enterprise, and if this in fact happened ... I believe prosecution of those who committed any of the acts and conduct in the conspiracy to defraud voters should be brought to justice,"[107]

Mayor Daley's Chicago, 1972. The Chicago Tribune was the 1973 winner of a Pulitzer Prize for local general or spot news reporting for uncovering flagrant violations of voting procedures in the primary election of March 21, 1972. The first in the series of articles this was first published on September 10, 1972 on widespread election fraud in Cook County and Daley's Chicago. The sting uncovered 838 elections code violations in 572 of the city's 3205 precincts. The brainchild of Chicago Tribune writer William Mullen, he arranged to be placed undercover as a clerk for the Board of Elections.

The Tribune realized they had a goldmine of investigative journalism and hatched a plan in 1972 to get 20 of its reporters to become precinct officials so they could see the machine from the inside. They observed countless cases of workers illegally helping voters and distributing partisan literature. Vote buying including chain voting (give a subverted voter a pre-marked ballot, have that voter vote and get a blank ballot, start the process over)[108] was done openly.

Some election observers had been threatened with death. Others were simply refused permission to observe. The livelihood of the party-appointed precinct captains was based on the votes they delivered. Each had a quota that differed in different precincts based on past history, and each had to deliver their quota or lose their job. Counts were regularly falsified. Democrat party bosses controlled all the election judge appointments.

In the legal article in the series, Tribune reporter Joel S. Summer wrote, "Because of the limited nature of the investigation, it was speculated that only a small percentage of the infractions had been discovered and reported to the public."[109] But the scandal was created and some cleanup of the Daley machine finally occurred after the Chicago Tribune published its series. The Illinois General Assembly passed and the Governor signed eight laws to get Chicago under control and over 40 indictments were filed for election fraud.

Kennedy vs. Nixon, 1960. This story starts with the Kennedy Nixon election in 1960. It is generally accepted—by Republicans with a groan and Democrats with a wink—that Nixon actually won the election in 1960. I'm old enough to remember, at eight, hanging leaflets on door knockers that year and have a vague recollection of watching the debates on our new, but still black and white TV. Eisenhower was still the President and respected by members of both parties. The 1960 election was fascinating to me as the first one I paid attention to. It is still fascinating now in the context of election fraud.

Democrats will tell you that the Nixon/Kennedy story was an urban myth. Joy-Ann Reid, a Republican-hater from way back, calls it a cruel myth, and claims, "the roots of the Republican obsession with voter fraud can be traced to the 1960 presidential election, which in GOP folklore was stolen from Dick Nixon for John F. Kennedy by Chicago Mayor Richard Daley."[110]

But is it not a myth. The 1960 presidential campaign between future Presidents John Kennedy and Richard Nixon turned out to be among the most controversial in modern memory. It was a contest between acknowledged friends and Senate colleagues. Interestingly, after his election President Kennedy and Senator Barry Goldwater, also friends, would have lunch weekly and engage in their favorite discussion—how much fun it would be for them to debate each other on the issues in their expected upcoming race 1964. Perhaps modern politics might have been much different—and less toxic—if the election had been between those two, cordially debating the issues, rather than what it was, between Goldwater and machine politician Lyndon Johnson with his daisy ad.

The JFK/RMN campaign was the closest popular vote ever seen in the modern US, with Kennedy winning by only 100,000 votes nationally out of the more than 68 Million votes cast, even closer he won Illinois by only 9,000 votes.

It will never be certain that Richard Nixon actually won both Texas and Illinois, the states he would have needed to secure the Electoral College vote. However, it is generally accepted in political science research circles that massive vote fraud was perpetrated on Kennedy's behalf in both states. Kennedy's margin of victory was 46,000 votes in Texas and Lyndon Johnson's Lone Star State political machine had the reputation for shenanigans that could easily produce that kind of margin. In Illinois, Chicago's infamous Mayor Daley, held back the Chicago vote until results from rural Republican Illinois came in late in the evening. Significantly behind, he then provided an unbelievable 450,000 margin of victory for Chicago and Cook County. All of that was needed; the final count had Kennedy leading by only 8,858 votes. With Kennedy in the White House and his brother Robert as Attorney General, and with Democrats Otto Kerner, Jr. and Price Daniel firmly in the state houses of

Illinois and Texas, respectively, no thorough investigation of the massive irregularities would ever be conducted. Who won is still a matter of conjecture and debate among the aging supporters of each President. It will likely never be known. [111]

What is known is that Vice President Nixon did not decide to contest the 1960 election. According Peter Flanigan, Nixon supporter and eventual appointee during Nixon's presidency, "Nixon emphatically said he would not challenge the results. And he did more than that. He told all of us on the staff to have no part of any challenge, and he sent back donations, all of them unsolicited, which were sent to finance a challenge."[112]

Some challenges did go on, though. Nixon supporters challenged the results in Illinois, Texas and nine other states. The Kennedy team challenged the results in Hawaii, and succeeded getting an additional three electoral votes there. A large part of the vote cast in Alabama in 1960 is routinely assigned to Kennedy. However these votes were for electors rather than directly for the Kennedy, whom they publicly did not support. [113]

Steven Schiller was at the time a 23 year old law student in special prosecutor Mo Wexler's office investigating the outcome of 1960 election. Schiller, now a retired judge thinks now that

Daley's Democratic Party mechanism was in place and, looking at the margin of victory, "it's very hard to believe that there wasn't at least a significant likelihood that the outcome would have been different in the state."[114]

Republican strategist Roger Stone recounts that by special prosecutor Mo Wexler's own report which came out in the spring of 1961 Wexler stated there was evidence of "substantial" miscounts in the more than 1300 precincts examined. Among Wexler's findings: unqualified voters; "misread" voting machines; and math mistakes. In one precinct there was even a drawing for hams. Despite the popular saying that there is no such thing as a free lunch, one precinct captain handed out slips of paper entitling voters to just that, a free lunch.

The evidence of vote fraud in Texas was as pervasive and dirty as Daley's Chicago style. The Kennedy ticket carried Texas by only 50,000 votes. Stone explains that thousands of Texas ballots were tossed out on a technicality because Texas voters did not scratch out the names of the candidates that they did not want, as Texas law required. (Sounds similar to the technicalities used to throw out the overseas military ballots in Florida 2000). To muddy the election waters further, not all counties applied the scratch out requirement. Lyndon Johnson himself was no stranger to election stealing. His first campaign for Senate was dogged by findings that he had stuffed ballot boxes, and caused other ballot boxes to "disappear" thus defeating the more conservative primary challenger, Democrat Governor Coke Stevenson. In Angelina County, in just one precinct results show that only 86 people voted in the 1960 Presidential election, yet the final tally gave 147 votes for Kennedy.[115]

So did Kennedy steal the election? We'll never know. Like Chappaquiddick and the grassy knoll, it is just another Kennedy mystery. Is this election the basis, as Joy-Ann claims, for the Republican obsession with vote fraud? Possibly, but who can blame them? As the patient said to the psychiatrist, "Just because I'm paranoid doesn't mean they're not out to get me." The Kennedy election in 1960 is certainly a scintillating data point among many that seems to suggest that Democrats will use fraud to get their end. As the Chicago Tribune wrote in its article on the electoral board's certification of the 1960 Illinois election, "Once an election has been stolen in Cook County, it stays stolen."[116]

13. Reforming the process

The Americans will always do the right thing...
After they've exhausted all the alternatives.—
Winston Churchill[117], British Prime Minister during
WWII

Democratic Party election fraud is not just a tool to be used by Democrats against Republicans but by Democrats against other Democrats challenging the party machine. Former President Jimmy Carter was certainly aware of the affect election fraud could have on the fairness of the election process. Carter's first race for public office in 1962 challenged Homer Moore, the candidate picked by the local political boss, Joe Hurst. In that race, Carter saw the effects of voter suppression, intimidation, and fraud. Carter lost that race initially due to ballot stuffing but, after successful battles in court, eventually emerged victorious. In his book, Turning Point, Carter writes, "The events of the 1962 campaign opened my eyes not only to the ways in which democratic processes can be subverted, but also to the capacity of men and women of good will to engage the System to right such wrongs."[118]

Carter was a good choice to be co-chairman of the Commission on Federal Election Reform, created in the aftermath of the 2000 Florida Bush-Gore debacle, as was his co-chair former

U.S. Secretary of State James A. Baker III. Both men had a reputation for working across the political aisle, both had honorable reputations, both had worked together to monitor the 1996 elections in Nicaragua,[119] and both were regarded as accomplished and ethical former senior members of government.

The commission issued a report in 2005[120] with 87 recommendations, including Voter ID and regular scrubbing of the election registration rolls. In the introductory letter from the co-chairs, Carter and Baker wrote, "Some Americans will prefer some of our proposals to others. Indeed, while all of the Commission members endorse the judgments and general policy thrust of the report in its entirety, they do not necessarily support every word and recommendation. Benefitting from Commission members with diverse perspectives, we have proposed, for example, a formula for transcending the sterile debate between integrity and access. Twenty-four states now require identification for voters, with some systems likely to restrict registration. We are recommending a photo ID system for voters designed to increase registration with a more affirmative and aggressive role for states in finding new voters and providing free IDs for those without driver's licenses. The formula we recommend will result in both more integrity and more access."[121] Before the ink was even dry on the report, the Democratic Party and supporting media began a barrage of vitriol, describing Voter ID as controversial (despite opinion polls consistently showing over 80 percent of voters in favor of Voter ID)[122] and overtly political.

Somehow lost in the furor over Voter ID were some of the other recommendations, including a universal registration system at the state rather than local level, combined with interoperability between states' lists to help states "remove interstate duplicates and help states to maintain an up-to-date, fully accurate registration list. This would mean people would need to register only once in their lifetime, and it would be easy to update their registration information when they move."[123] The Commission recommended uniform procedures for counting provisional ballots. The Commission's recommendation for Voter ID was that there would less opportunity for discrimination with a single, uniform ID than if poll workers "can apply multiple standards". The commission recommended a number of ways for states to make registration more convenient and facilitate voting by overseas military and civilians. Other recommendations included standards for electronic voting machines, including a paper back up to allow audits and thus ensure confidence in the count, non-partisan state-wide election commissions. Finally the Commission reviewed the implementation of HAVA and noted that it would take years longer than mandated to be fully implemented and that state-wide voter databases, in particular would be completed significantly beyond the 1 January 2006 deadline.

As far as election fraud is concerned, the Commission wrote, "The U.S. Department of Justice has launched more than 180 investigations into election fraud since October 2002. The investigations have resulted in charges being brought against 89 individuals and in convictions of 52 individuals for multiple voting, providing false information on their felon status, and other offenses. The convictions related to a variety of election fraud offenses, from vote buying to submitting false voter registration information and voting-related offenses by non-citizens." ... "In addition to the federal investigations, state attorneys general and local prosecutors handle cases of election fraud. Other cases are never pursued because of the difficulty in obtaining sufficient evidence for prosecution or because of the low priority given to election fraud cases. One district attorney, for example, explained that he did not pursue allegations of fraudulent voter registration because that is a victimless and nonviolent crime."

The report notes, "Election fraud usually attracts public attention and comes under investigation only in close elections." The report then goes on to say, "When there is a wide margin, the losing candidate rarely presses for an investigation." Fraud in any degree and in any circumstance is subversive to the electoral process. The best way to maintain ballot integrity is to investigate all credible allegations of election fraud and otherwise prevent fraud before it can affect an election."

The Commission went on to cite evidence of absentee ballot and voter registration fraud. "Fraud occurs in several ways. Absentee ballots remain the largest source of potential vote fraud. A notorious recent case of absentee ballot fraud occurred in Miami's mayoral election of 1998, and in that case, the judge declared the election fraudulent and called for a new election. Absentee balloting is vulnerable to abuse in several ways: Blank ballots mailed to the wrong address or to large residential buildings might get intercepted. Citizens who vote at home, at nursing homes, at the workplace, or in church are more susceptible to pressure, overt and subtle, or to intimidation. Vote buying schemes are far more difficult to detect when citizens vote by mail."

The Commission noted fraud in the 1996 California Sanchez/Dornan congressional election (784 invalid votes), 200 non-citizen registrations in a random check in Honolulu in 2000, and non-citizens applying for and receiving voter cards in Maryland and Texas in 2004. The report warned of the growth of unofficial voter registration drives, often conducted by paid workers, causing increased voter registration fraud and cited accusations being investigated in 10 states stemming from the 2004 election and 19 US federal prosecutions for voter registration fraud.

As regards investigation and prosecution of election fraud, the Commission made several recommendations: the Department of Justice, each state's attorney general, and local prosecutor should issue a public report in the even years on its investigations of election fraud to include the numbers of allegations made, matters investigated, cases prosecuted, and individuals convicted for various crimes; the Department of Justice should increase staff to investigate and prosecute election and fraud; it should be a "federal felony to engage in any act of violence, property destruction", "or threatened act of violence" to lawful right to vote or participate in a federal election; and the enactment of "legislation to prohibit any individual or group from deliberately providing the public with incorrect information about election procedures for the purpose of preventing voters from going to the polls."[124] This recommendation clearly addressed the 2000 Bush/Gore Florida Panhandle disinformation campaign. Regarding the problems of absentee voting fraud, the

Commission recommended a prohibition of third party "organizations, candidates, and political party activists from handling absentee ballots" and recommended that absentee ballots received before Election Day be kept secure.[125]

So, does election fraud exist? This commission seemed to think so and they believed it to be damaging enough to our democracy that measures were required to insure that it be curtailed. Demand for fair and fraud-free elections is not a Republican obsession but a bi-partisan call to ensure the integrity of our electoral system. Voter fraud is a national disgrace and responsible leaders from both political parties agree.

Incomplete or inaccurate registration lists lie at the root of many problems encountered in U.S. elections. When a voter list omits the names of citizens who believe they properly registered or contains incorrect or out-of-date information on registered voters, eligible citizens often are denied the right to vote. Invalid voter files, which contain ineligible, duplicate, fictional, or deceased voters, are an invitation to fraud. Creating computer accessible voter rolls, keeping them up to date, creating non-partisan state-wide election commissions, and requiring positive identification to ensure the voter is who he or she says he is will fix much of the fraud. Ensuring easy registration and proper and timely handling of absentee ballots should stamp out most of the rest of the fraud as well as ensuring that all eligible voters can do so and have their vote counted.

14. Obama—hoping to block change

I took an oath to protect the people of Arizona, and that's what I'm going to do. I'm going to keep pushing in that direction.—Jan Brewer[126], Arizona Governor

Just because the Carter-Baker Commission recommended it; just because NVRA (Motor Voter), HAVA, and MOVE require it; just because it's the right thing to do, doesn't mean that the Obama Administration isn't going to try to stop it. Again and again as we move toward the November 2012 election, we see attempts to prohibit Voter ID, stop cleanup of registration rolls, and block our troops from voting. Here are just a few examples.

Arizona citizenship proof required for voter registration Arizona, a state with a high percent of illegal aliens, passed a voter-approved initiative in 2004, which among other things required proof of citizenship to register to vote.[127] After several years of back and forth in the courts the US Ninth Circuit struck down the provision, since the requirement is not part of the Motor Voter law, and the Supreme Court upheld the 9th Circuit decision in June 2012. But it's not as simple as that. Under federal preemption, the ruling only applies the Federal form. Arizona can still ask for proof of citizenship if the state form is used—and the state does not have to tell the potential voter about the federal form. The state also has the right to examine Voter ID, which requires proof of citizenship, at the polling place prior to voting no matter which registration form was executed. The upshot? There will be more illegals on the registration rolls, more opportunities for fraud, and more lawsuits contesting the outcomes of elections.[128]

DHS blocked Florida's use of data. For several months in 2012, the Obama/Holder Department of Justice frantically blocked Florida from purging its rolls of ineligible and obsolete voters, including non-citizens and dead. At the same time, the Obama Department of Homeland Security refused to allow Florida to access its Systematic Alien Verification for Entitlements (SAVE) database, as mandated by the Motor Voter, which requires states to remove ineligible voters to clean up the rolls and the Federal Government to provide data to help them do so.

While waiting for eventual access, Florida used its DMV records and contacted each questioned voter within 30 days to determine if the name should be removed. If the name was removed, the voter could still vote provisionally, just in case there was an error.[129]

Florida was of course highly criticized for using its DMV records for the process, because it was a less accurate system than SAVE. So why did Florida not use the much more accurate (SAVE) database—because the Department of Homeland Security wouldn't give it to them, of course. In responding to the accusations, Governor Rick Scott explained "We know we have almost a hundred individuals that are registered to vote that are not U.S. citizens," adding that "I have an obligation to enforce the laws of our land" that has been compromised because "Homeland Security has been stonewalling, [so] we have no choice but to sue." He went on to complain that Florida had done "all the right things," and had not purged anyone from the registration rolls, and still wanted the SAVE database to check more accurate citizen data.[130]

In contravention to Federal Law, Department of Homeland Security refused to share that data with Florida, and with Colorado, both of which had been trying to access the information for over a year. (Arizona had also been denied access to SAVE because they were trying to mandate employers to use E-Verify to determine employment eligibility).

When asked about the database, Governor Rick Scott said, "The statute says that the state has a right to use that database for voter registration. That's the law," he went on to say, "We'll make sure that we do it the right way. Not one U.S. citizen has been eliminated from the voter rolls. Not one."[131] Florida eventually won the suit for access guaranteed to them by Federal law so that the state could scrub voter registration files as Florida was required to do by Federal law. So what is SAVE and how accurate is it? According testimony by Department of Homeland Security in a recent Supreme Court case, Chamber of Commerce of the United States v. Whiting, E-Verify has less than 0.3% error rate. Using the SAVE system (E-Verify data), immigration status can be determined in 3-5 seconds for 90% of cases.[132] Combined with Florida's provisional voting provisions, the use of the SAVE database means Florida can ensure a nearly alien-free registration, as required by both Federal and State Laws.

15. Voter ID & clean registrations

The greatness of America lies not in being more enlightened than any other nation, but rather in her ability to repair her faults.—Alexis de Tocqueville[133], Political Theorist

It is a typical Democratic argument that Voter ID requirements are biased against minority voters. Claims are often made that it suppresses the vote—statistics pointed out elsewhere in this book show that that is no true. In Texas, at least, statistics show that it does not place a disproportionate burden on those potential voters either. In fact in a recently released article, University of Texas professor Daron Shaw wrote that 1.9% of white voters, 1.23% of African American voters, and 0.96% of Hispanic voters would require voter id to be issued to vote.[134] These numbers are not statistically very different and are actually biased in favor of those minorities. So why do Democrats oppose Voter ID? As we have no doubt incessantly repeated the point so many times, Voter ID and clean voter rolls make it harder to vote other people's registrations. And that's been part of the Democrats ground game for over a century; old (and dead) dogs will need to learn new tricks.

Other surveys show similar things. An American University study found that in

Maryland, Indiana, and Mississippi less than 0.05 percent of registered voters were without government-issued ID and concluded that a photo ID did not appear to be a serious problem in any of these states. In a similar study conducted in 2006, 36,000 voters were sampled and only 23 were found to be without ID. To answer arguments that even such a small number must not be denied the right to vote, it should be noted that every state that has passed a Voter ID law has procedures for provisional voting—unidentified voters are not turned away at the polls. [135]

In a follow up on a survey in Indiana in 2006, the Carter-Baker Commission on Election Reform observed that "contrary to the fears of opponents of the law, [the Commission] did not find confusion at the polls or evidence of citizens being prevented from voting because they did not have IDs." The report went on to say that Indiana had implemented an "excellent public education program, voters were aware of the new law and were not bothered by having to bring IDs to the polls".[136]

The Brennan Center, a left leaning think tank opposed to Voter ID, claims that the numbers are much higher, but they get that number by not asking if the respondent had government-issued ID, but whether they had readily available identification and asking if their US birth certificate or naturalization papers were in a place where they could access them today or tomorrow. Since these things are often kept in safe places, such as a bank safe deposit box, the questions clearly are intended to solicit a higher percentage than asking if they had an ID card. And, since elections are scheduled with significant advance notice, the poll did not really get to the point of whether they could get an ID in time to vote.[137]

NBC Newsman, Chris Matthews, supported Voter ID a few years ago. But now that he thinks it might help Republicans, he piously opposes it on moral grounds. On 20 July 2011 Matthews said, no doubt in a weak moment of uncharacteristic honesty, "Because they—and I know this goes on. It has gone on in old-time politics. It has gone on since the '50s that I know about. People call up, see if you voted or you're not going to vote. The, all of a sudden, somebody does come and vote for you. This is an old strategy in big city politics." He went on to say, "I know all about it in North Philly. It's what went on. And I believe it still goes on. The question is, can we correct it without screwing up our system? I want people to vote, that's the number one goal. But I also want to make sure people don't cheat. So, let's get out of here." But barely one year later, he jumped on the anti-Voter ID bandwagon by criticizing Mike Turasi, PA State House Majority Leader's statement that cracking down on vote fraud "is going to allow Governor Romney to win the state of Pennsylvania." Matthews then said that Voter ID was nothing but a plot to "kill off the older voters and others who might be planning, how dare they, to vote for Obama."[138] Unintentionally, Matthews made it very clear that opposition to Voter ID is a totally partisan activity. Bah!

Subsequently, Pennsylvania won in state court this August, when that court rejected a suit by the ACLU to block the Pennsylvania's Voter ID law from coming into effect. The US Supreme court had previously upheld a similar statute in Indiana. When asked why the Pennsylvania ACLU had taken its case to the state courts, spokesman Witold Walczak, said, "going into federal court is like going to the plate with two strikes already against you." Undeterred by the state court decision, Obama's Justice Department launched an inquiry into the state's Voter ID law, despite the fact that Pennsylvania is not one of the states subject to pre-clearance under Section 5 of the Voting Rights Act. In response to what appeared to be a fishing expedition, James Schultz, the Pennsylvania General Council, wrote, "In light of the absence of authority for your request for information, I question whether your inquiry is truly motivated by a desire to assess compliance with federal voting rights laws, or rather is fueled by political motivation," And so continues the

Democrats' war to keep the door open for voter substitution fraud.[139]

In Kansas, data filed by the Secretary state showed that only 32 of the state's 1.7 million voters requested free IDs upon the passing of the requirement in 2011. One reason for such a low request rate are the numerous existing forms of identification accepted at the polls, including: "a driver's license issued by Kansas or by another state or district of the United States; a state identification card issued by Kansas or by another state or district of the United States; a concealed carry handgun license issued by Kansas or a concealed carry handgun or weapon license issued by another state or district of the United States; a United States passport; an employee badge or identification document issued by a municipal, county, state, or federal government office or agency; a military identification document issued by the United States; a student identification card issued by an accredited postsecondary institution of education in the state of Kansas; a public assistance identification card issued by a municipal, county, state, or federal government office or agency; or an identification card issued by an Indian tribe". The law further exempts military and overseas citizens voting under UOCAVA, those with religious objections to photographic IDs, and those with disabilities that prevent them from travelling. Voters over 65 may use an expired ID. Similar requirements exist for requesting absentee ballots.[140]

One of the sanctioned states under the 1965 Voting Rights Act, Georgia sought and received pre-clearance for its Voter ID program, which it implemented in 2007 after receiving pre-clearance from the Department of Justice. Georgia's ID requirements were similar to that of Kansas; acceptable ID included: "a Georgia driver's license, even if expired, or a Georgia photo Voter ID card; any state or federal government-issued photo ID (which includes a student ID issued by the Georgia state college system); a U.S. passport; an employee photo ID from any branch or department of the federal government or Georgia state or local government; a U.S. military photo ID; or a tribal photo ID. Given the state's history of discrimination, Georgia launched as significant education campaign, which included sending 5 Million pieces of direct mail and inserts into utility bills and over 36 Million informational brochures to be offered at churches, libraries, etc. throughout Georgia. Perhaps because of the publicity, Georgia issued 26,506 free Voter ID cards from 2006 through early 2012, less than half a percent of registered, active voters. During this process, a group including the ALCU and NCAAP filed an ultimately unsuccessful suit against Georgia, charging voter suppression.

Statistics belie this claim. Comparing the 2004 and 2008 presidential campaigns, Hispanic voter turnout in Georgia increased by 140%, African American turnout increased by 42%, and white turnout increased by 85% . Comparing the 2006 and 2008 mid-term elections, the numbers again showed no bias against minorities; increases were: Hispanic 66.5%; African American 44.2%; and White 11.7%.[141]

Voter ID Upheld by US Supreme Court. The Supreme Court ruled in Crawford v Marion County Election Board in 2008 by a 6-3 vote to uphold an Indiana law requiring voters to present a photo identification, finding that the Indiana law did not violate the US Constitution. All nine justices rejected the argument that requiring a photo id disenfranchised voters. Under Indiana law a voter lacking a photo ID can vote a provisional ballot. To have the provisional ballot count, the voter would need to show a valid ID within ten days of the election at a designated state government location, or sign a statement saying that they could not afford a photo ID. For its part Indiana said there were virtually no problems and the state had conducted six elections using the Voter ID rules while Democrats argued that Indiana's law disenfranchised "hundreds of thousands of voters, including a disproportionate number of minority, elderly and poor people. Indiana did not charge for its Voter ID cards. That fact alone may have clinched the Supreme Court victory, especially since the prosecution could not provide anyone to the court that was unable to obtain a Voter ID due to cost.

The Supreme Court agreed to hear the case after the District Court and the Seventh Circuit Court of Appeals both upheld the Indiana law. The Circuit Court however was deeply divided and in its dissent the court wrote that the Voter ID law was a "thinly veiled attempt to disenfranchise low income democratic voters." Amid these charges of Republican partisanship the court still found that the Indiana laws neutral justifications "should not be disregarded simply because partisan interests may have provided one motivation for the votes of individual legislators." The court was deciding not on a specific instance, but for problems that could come up in the long term.

The leading Supreme Court opinion was written by Justice John Paul Stevens who wrote that the burden placed on the voter, represented a very small minority compared to the state's interest in reducing vote fraud. He wrote: "Because Indiana's cards are free, the inconvenience of going to the Bureau of Motor Vehicles, gathering required documents, and posing for a photograph does not qualify as a substantial burden on most voters' right to vote, or represent a significant increase over the usual burdens of voting." [142] Voter ID is a now requirement in more than thirty states.

Cleaning up the voter rolls. We have come to expect politicians to lie and advocate totally false, misleading and contradictory positions. However the Democrats' position on Voter ID is really beyond credibility to anyone. The Democrats claim that Voter ID is a poll tax—yet in no state where Voter ID has been implemented does a Voter ID cost anything.

The Democrats claim that voter roll purging will prevent eligible voters from voting—yet in all states scrubbing their data, a voter whose registration was purged in error can vote provisionally and confirm information in case the provisional ballot is needed to determine election outcome. The Democrats claim that purging the dead, felons, and non-citizens discriminate against racial minorities—yet none of those purged are allowed to vote anyway and no minority eligible to vote is purged

The Democrats claim that voter roll purge and Voter ID are only supported by Republicans—yet they are both things strongly recommended by the Commission on Federal Election Reform, co-chaired by former President Jimmy Carter and Former Secretary of State James A. Baker III after the difficulties encountered in the 2000 election. The Democrats claim that there is no vote fraud—yet there is documented history stretching back into the 19th century in America of consistent and regular vote fraud—committed in general by Democrats in urban areas, by unions in labor elections, and by Republicans in rural areas.

Judge confirms Florida's right to purge voter rolls. On 6 June 2012, after months of attempts by the Department of Justice to block Florida's efforts to comply with both Federal and State law by purging, dead, felons, and felons from the voter rolls, US District Judge Robert Hinkle confirmed Florida's contention that federal laws did not prevent Florida from complying with Federal laws. In letter pointing out the Judge's ruling to Attorney General Eric Holder, Representative Tom Rooney (FL-16) wrote, "Your department also alleges that the removal violates Section 8 of the National Voter Registration Act, which prohibits the removal of names from voter registration rolls within 90 days of an election. This claim is also false. Section 8 applies to previously eligible voters who have become ineligible for certain reasons, like moving out of state. It does not apply to voters who have become ineligible through death, criminal conviction, or mental capacity. Section 8 does not apply to voters who were ineligible at the time they registered, which is a felony, including noncitizens."[143]

16. Fighting fraud in Wisconsin—a model for victory

Some WI Democrats [are] crying voter fraud.
Apparently some Republicans had been going
around locking cemetery gates.—Fred Thompson[144]
, former US Senator (R-TN)

The Wisconsin 2012 Recall election on 5 Jun 2012 was a triumph for the Republican Party in several ways. Clearly the victory vindicated Governor Scott Walker's tough stance taken to wrest control of government pay and benefits away from the state's public employee unions. But it was as much a triumph of a well planned and executed Republican ground game against the Democratic Party, usually thought of as establishing the *sine qua non* of American political tactics. Democrats are known for tough, often dirty, electoral politics. Even when weak on issues, their legions of foot soldiers provided by union members and college students usually swamp the efforts of telephone banks of Republican blue hairs in both energy and effectiveness.

In Wisconsin the recall was expected to have an unprecedented number of Democratic Party foot soldiers. The election would be on an important union issue, viewed as nothing less than union busting by the public employee union bosses, and would have national ramifications. The stakes were high and the hopes were high for a Democratic victory in a state carried by 14 percentage points by Obama in 2008. Milwaukee Democratic partisans were famous for producing enough votes from dead and duplicate voters. Indeed, on Election Day, out of state unions bussed in thousands of union members to get out the Democratic vote.

But the Republican Party was coming off a surprising turnaround of fortunes in 2010; they had elected Governor Scott Walker (R) and Tea Party supported US Senator Rod Johnson (R). The Republicans attracted significant expenditures, both for the campaign and via independent groups, with the Republicans outspending the Democrats on the order of $45 Million to $18 Million.[145] However, unlike many Republican campaigns in the past, the Republican Party also launched an outstanding ground game—a combined get out the vote campaign and Republican sponsorship of election monitoring.

The Republican recall get-out-the-vote campaign in Wisconsin was nothing short of tremendous. More than two dozen campaign offices were opened, all of which were transferred to the Romney campaign just days after victory. Republicans courted early absentee voters and ran an outstanding online campaign buying ads on Google, Facebook, and YouTube. In 2010, the Wisconsin Republican Party had made about 2 Million voter contacts. For the recall, that number was nearly 5 Million. The RNC experimented with using out of state Republicans to make phone calls to Wisconsin voters—a tactic that worked so well that it will be repeated for the November 2012 election using non-battleground state Republicans to call into targeted battleground states.

Using its non-partisan allied group, We're Watching Wisconsin Elections, Republicans were able to insure that legions of trained election observers manned the polls, residential care facilities, and central count locations in order to combat or forestall attempts at election fraud.[146] More will be discussed about this in the final chapter, A Call to Action. With a close election expected in November 2012, preventing election fraud may be more important to winning than the issues in this era of millions of dead and duplicate registered voters.

All in all, Wisconsin was a Republican pilot for the November 2012 election. A dynamite ground game using social media and using technology to direct available volunteer resources to key races combined with allied groups to fight election fraud is a winning strategy.[147]

17. Taking measures

From tea parties to the election in Massachusetts,
we are witnessing the single greatest political
pushback in American history.—Marco Rubio[148],
US Senator (R-FL)

So, before we move to the last chapter, A Call to Action, what have we learned so far? Vote fraud in the United States goes back to the very beginning of our republic. Its use, more or less successfully, has been consistent in all major elections at least since the mid-1900s. There is little sign of Democrats abandoning the tactic. Yet Democrats claim again and again that there is no voter fraud and so there should be no effort made to prevent it. "Pay no attention to the man behind the curtain!"[149]

Neither party can claim absolute purity in their conduct when it comes to fraud free and fair elections. However, election fraud as an accepted practice is a Democratic Party ploy, not a Republican one.

Traditionally, urban Democrats and their foot soldiers, the unions, have used registration fraud, voter intimidation, substitution fraud, and counting fraud as regular parts of their ground game to win elections. As we showed in President Jimmy Carter's early political experience, electoral fraud has also been used by Democrats against Democrats, in particular in their old stronghold, the South.

Historically, Republican vote fraud has been generally rural, isolated, and small time with the possible exception of Illinois in the 1960s, when rural Republicans engaged in pretty extensive efforts in statewide elections to counteract known fraud in Chicago and Cook County.

Despite the drumbeat of Democratic Party accusations, voter suppression is not the Republican version of election fraud. Suppression of minorities and the poor from voting can be directly traced to the re-establishment of Democratic political control in the south at the end of Reconstruction. It was white southern Democrats that implemented the Jim Crow laws of the era, and it was bi-partisan action in the Congress that implemented the Voting Rights act in 1965 and action by the Supreme Court that outlawed the last vestiges of Jim Crow at the same time. In fact, substantially larger Republican majorities in the House and Senate voted for the Voting Rights Act than did Democrats, where some old southern democrats still resisted.

Voter fraud is facilitated by registration rolls bloated with obsolete registrations—voters that have died, have moved, or are ineligible to vote for reasons such as being a non-citizen or felon. It has been proven that Democratic Party supporting organizations, such as ACORN, conducted mass efforts (often funded by illegally diverted Federal funds) to stuff the rolls with illegal registrations. And, despite laws such as Motor Voter and HAVA that require the states to clean up their voter rolls, Democrats have made it a strategy to oppose removing these non-voters from the rolls and, most recently, have used the Department of Justice to make attempts to block legally required efforts by the states to do so.

Voter ID makes it harder to commit vote fraud. Voter ID statutes have been declared constitutional in Indiana and several other states by the US Supreme Court. Yet the Department of Justice is blocking the exact same statutes wherever it can. Why? They claim it is voter suppression and tantamount to a poll tax. Yet the court ruled that it was not and statistics support this. So why do the Democrats persist in this claim? Because without Voter ID it is easier to vote the false, inaccurate, and dead registrations, the removal of which the Department of Justice is also attempting to block.

It has always been difficult for military posted overseas to vote. However, there have also been efforts made to improve this over the past 80 years or so. Unfortunately, overseas military voters remain largely disenfranchised, although registered at a rate higher than the general population. In the last few federal election cycles, only a few percent have been able to cast their votes in time to have them count. Many, if not most, of the ballots sent late to our overseas military voters are from Democratic Party controlled states and counties. Clearly in the election of 2000, Democratic lawyers in the state of Florida strategically targeted rejection of military overseas ballots in what turned out to be a desperate attempt to change the Florida results via recount.

Hard fought legislation such as MOVE has resulted in a one stop federal website where overseas military can request registration and ballot materials on the Internet via a standard form valid in all states. For some states, military and overseas voters can return registration, ballot requests, and even ballots electronically. And, if timely ballots are not received, there is now the Federal Write-in Absentee ballot (FWAB), printable via Internet, accepted by all states and territories for all federal candidates and for many states for state and local candidates and ballot measures. This is very significant progress, but our overseas military must be educated about the new procedures encouraged to vote the new ballots. Election monitors must be there to make sure the states and counties count them.

The Commission on Federal Election Reform, created in the aftermath of the 2000 Bush-Gore debacle, was co-chaired by former U.S. President Jimmy Carter and former U.S. Secretary of State James A. Baker III. The commission issued a report in 2007 with 87 recommendations, including Voter ID and regular scrubbing of the election registration rolls. Demand for fair and fraud-free elections is not a Republican plot but a bi-partisan call to ensure the integrity of our electoral system. Highlighted among the recommendations were state-level organization and updating of registration lists, national interoperability to prevent duplication when voters move, the use of REAL ID cards or state-issued photo ID for non-drivers at polls, and voter-verifiable paper audit trails for electronic voting machines. Voter fraud is a national disgrace and responsible leaders from both political parties agree.

Lack of Poll Workers. By some estimates in 2012 the United States has a shortage of half a million poll watchers. The passing of the World War II generation, the Greatest Generation as Tom Brokaw put it, has left a profound shortage of dedicated, experienced poll workers. The shortage of poll watchers is so widespread that it has been frequently cited as the reason for voting irregularities. In Racine, Wisconsin officials blamed a shortage of poll workers for rampant fraud.

It has become increasingly difficult to staff the polls with workers. Being a poll worker doesn't pay much and typically poll workers have come from legions of older Americans, willing to work for a day as part of their civic duty with a few dollars as a nice upside for a very long day's work—often as long as fourteen hours. As the Greatest Generation has aged, fewer members of the succeeding generations have stepped up to do this work. In many cities there just are not enough poll workers from both parties to run a fair polling place.

In his book, Stealing Elections, John Fund told the story of Marsha Olney, a resident of Los Angeles County. Responding to county appeals for poll workers, she volunteered to work up to four hours during an upcoming Primary Election. Five days before the election, a truck pulled up to her home in Venice Beach and delivered voting machines and other equipment to run a polling place. The driver told her that she would be manning, by herself, a polling place at a nearby school for the whole Election Day. On that day, she drove to the school, unloaded the boxes, and set up the polling place. The first time since the drop off on Friday that the registrar's office contacted her was around noon, when a representative drove by the poll to make sure everything was OK. Marsha noted that there were no safeguards to prevent her from voting unused ballots, no audits, nothing.[150] She, of course, did her civic duty; ran a clean polling place; got the ballots where they needed to go. However, repeats of this problem occur more and more as those Americans that used to do poll work and election monitoring become too old for a grueling fourteen hour day.

Students at Berkeley were asked to become poll workers in the June 5th primary election in California. The Election Administration Research Center posted a request for Berkeley students to help out. The request says in part "Please consider helping out! You can sign up with a colleague, friend or neighbor and ask to be placed in the same polling place. *You can also recruit a group of people and run an entire polling place!* [italics mine][151]   It would be nice to find a Republican or two to join them as well.

In Springfield Ohio area election officials in Clark and Champaign counties found high school students to assist at precincts in the Ohio primary. The Springfield News Sun reported: "While only a handful of students are expected to work at precincts in Champaign County in March, officials in Clark County said that they received close to thirty volunteers.   Not all will work as poll workers, some will help unload ballots from vehicles on election night and others will help direct voters to the right precinct."[152]

Common Cause is actively recruiting its interns to work as poll watchers in the 2012 general election on their common blog website, "...there is great potential for young people to work at the polls. As voting systems modernize, young people will be more able to comprehend and explain these procedures fluently to voters."[153] The pitch is a bit hokey and ageist, appealing to youthful ego and earnestness. After all, the American workforce has been computer literate since the late 1980's. However it does show awareness that there are just not enough volunteers to ensure smooth and honest elections.

With Voter ID and more accurate registration rolls, the opportunity exists this year to run fair, fraud free elections—but only if, as in the Wisconsin Recall Election, there are enough volunteers to staff and monitor the election process.

As described earlier, organizations such as Republican-backed but non-partisan We're Watching Wisconsin Elections, are supplying poll workers and watchers. They clearly made a difference during the Wisconsin Recall of 2012, ensuring that no-widespread election fraud took hold in an election with significant potential or same.

As we approach the 2012 election various organizations are recognizing the need. Non-partisan organizations generally thought of as affiliating with the Democratic Party such as Common Cause are attempting to attract younger citizens to man the polls. Non-partisan organizations such as Tea Party-hatched True the Vote and Republican-supported organizations such as We're Watching Wisconsin Elections are researching voter rolls and will provide poll workers and watchers this November. Grass roots organizations, generally organized by Tea Partiers and Republicans, exemplified by such local organizations as Missouri's MOPP (Missouri Precinct Project)[154], are sprouting up all over the country.

Veterans groups are getting involved as well. Get Out the Vet is an organization founded by the author of this book, a Navy veteran with 36-years active and reserve service, and his wife, Janet Brink, who led the Reagan-Bush military get-out-the-vote campaign in 1984. Recruiting vets to help get out the overseas military vote and monitor the polls, Get Out the Vet aims both to ensure our military gets to vote and to provide election monitors to ensure a fair fraud-free election.

The reader can join in. Plan to take Election Day off. Volunteer to be a poll worker or election monitor. Help ensure a fair and fraud-free election.

18. A call to action!

Freedom is never more than one generation away from extinction. We didn't pass it to our children in the bloodstream. It must be fought for, protected, and handed on for them to do the same, or one day we will spend our sunset years telling our children and our children's children what it was once like in the United States where men were free.—Ronald Reagan[155], 40th President of the United States

This year the Obama campaign schemes and plans the greatest vote theft yet. The Obama Department of Justice stopped all efforts to clean up the voter rolls—until the courts said NO! Every new Voter ID law was challenged in the courts—even if it was modeled on ones previously allowed by the Supreme Court. Obama's Department of Homeland Security withheld information on alien residents, which would allow states to clean up their voter registration lists.

Pious Democrats tell us that any attempt to clean up the registration rolls or to require that a voter is really who s/he says he claims to be must be a racist attempt to suppress the vote of under privileged who need to vote to be adequately represented.

Defunct ACORN, resurrected under a myriad of other names to avoid Congressional funding, is up to its old fraudulent registration antics. The Democrats, concerned that their efforts to buy votes with money stolen from the people might not be enough—people who don't pay taxes don't show up to the polls either— continue to seek a special advantage—fraud. And incorrect voter rolls provide this in a major way.

Not satisfied just with enough dead, aliens, felons, and multiple registrations littering the registration rolls, the Obama Department of Justice continues its effort to disenfranchise our military by refusing to hold states and counties accountable for late ballot materials to out overseas troops.

In cities like St Louis, Chicago, Milwaukee, and Philadelphia all of the potential for election fraud exists and every type of fraud has occurred. Voter rolls are stuffed with dead, obsolete, duplicate registrations ripe for the picking. Busloads of paid voters have been carted to the polls. Election workers have voted unused registrations at the end of the day. Ballot tampering, missing ballots, and fraudulent counts have been the tools used to elect Democrats year in and year out. Ballots are counted, and if the favored candidate needs more votes they miraculously appear a few hours later.

Or, as in St. Louis in 2008, the polls can be held open until enough of the right votes come in.

I have laid out a history of fraud, irregularities, indictments, incompetence in managing out elections. It doesn't really matter, however, whether there is a lot of fraud or just a little. The issue, given the stakes involved, is to reduce or eliminate the opportunity to commit fraud. Only a few more votes miscounted, ballots altered, voters confused, or military disenfranchised in Florida (about a hundred) could have changed the outcome of the 2000 election. Or the involvement of the courts could have so damaged the legitimacy of the election that Al Gore, self-proclaimed inventor of the Internet and savior of the Earth, could have been President when we were attacked on 9/11 or our Commander in Chief could have been hamstrung in his reaction to that crisis.

Now consider the justification for regulation in our businesses—say financial—where there is no end to regulation to remove the potential for fraud. Consider government ethics rules, where gifts of more than $25 are forbidden to eliminate any perception of influence or fraud. Consider environmental regulation, where unproven risks are regulated away because of fears of unknown disaster.

So why should we permit a condition where there could be even the perception of fraud in an election? Having our votes count is a most fundamental liberty, not some politician's pet cause. We must have a balance between a fair and fraud-free election and ensuring that all eligible people can vote. Clean voter rolls, Voter ID, timely absentee ballots, and provisional voting accomplish that in theory. However we need citizens to man the polls as workers and election monitors to ensure that fairness is done and to provide needed oversight of our political parties and government officials.

The fraud and military voter disenfranchisement can be stopped and fair fraud-free elections can be guaranteed!

States like Florida and Texas have won in the courts and are now cleaning up their voter registration rolls. The Department of Homeland Security has given up its resistance and is providing data on resident aliens from the SAVE database to at least some states that have requested it.

As of this summer, 33 states have implemented or are implementing Voter ID laws. Six of the states are awaiting preclearance from the Department of Justice under Section 5 of the Voting Rights Act; Obama's Department of Justice has been resisting laws identical to those

147

already approved by the U.S Supreme Court and there may be hearings prior to the 2012 election:

9 states have laws requiring Strict Photo ID: 5 states—Georgia, Indiana, Kansas, Pennsylvania, and Tennessee—have implemented the law; 2 states—South Carolina and Texas—are awaiting preclearance under Section 5 of the Voting Rights Act; Wisconsin is appealing a State Supreme Court Ruling; and Mississippi has not yet implemented the law.

8 states have laws requiring Photo ID: 6 states—Florida, Hawaii, Idaho, Louisiana, Michigan, and South Dakota—have implemented the law; Alabama and New Hampshire are awaiting preclearance.

3 states have laws requiring Strict Non-Photo ID: Arizona and Ohio have implemented the law; Virginia is awaiting preclearance.

13 states have laws requiring Non-Strict Non-Photo ID: Alaska, Arkansas, Colorado, Connecticut, Delaware, Kentucky, Missouri, Montana, North Dakota, Oklahoma, Rhode Island, Utah, and Washington. Rhode Island will implement a Photo ID requirement in time for the 2014 elections.[156]

The Federal Voting Assistance Program (FVAP) has received significant funding under the MOVE Act and has made great strides since 2010

148

in providing a one-stop voting portal for our overseas military and civilian voters at fvap.org. Most states are making significant effort to remove barriers to military voting and provide ballots earlier.

Voter groups—both Republican and non-partisan—are researching voter rolls this year, checking names with the Social Security Death Index, scanning for duplicates for people that have moved.

All of this is good, but it means little unless there is a way to observe and challenge at the polls. We need poll workers. In cities like Los Angeles and St. Louis there are not even enough poll workers to run the polls. So the Democratic machine produces volunteers, all Democrat, to sit in for absent Republicans—just like the fox watching the henhouse. Republican volunteers must turn out to work the polls to monitor where the ballots go and make sure votes aren't stolen by other poll workers at the last moment.

We need election monitors. Armed with lists of suspicious registrations, Republican monitors must watch the election and challenge votes cast in the name of these bad registrations. In some states, they may request poll workers to issue provisional ballots. In other states, they will have to catalog the bad votes so that they can be protested later. In many places, the ballot number used is listed by the registration—so the specific bad ballot can be identified during the count.

Lots of volunteers are needed. There are about 175,000 precincts, and a slightly similar number of polling places, in the US. If we can watch all of them, it will significantly reduce the possibility of fraud. If we make it known that this is happening, it may reduce the incentive for committing fraud in the first place. That could make the Democrat's claim that vote fraud is a myth into a reality.

Voter assistance programs and organizations

Every election is determined by the people who show up.—Larry Sabato[157], Professor, UVA

There are a number of organizations that have been effective assisting overseas military voters and in fighting vote fraud. A much abbreviated list of just a few of them is here.

Federal Voter Assistance Program: (www.fvap.gov) The FVAP is an official Department of Defense agency mandated to assist all military and overseas civilian voters to register to vote, request absentee ballots, and vote. Organized in 1956, the FVAP also monitors and reports State compliance with Federal voting laws and recommendations pertaining to military and overseas voting. Under the 2009 MOVE Act, the FVAP has an expanded budget and reporting mandate. The FVAP website includes a portal for registration and voting in all US states and territories.

Overseas Vote Foundation: (www.overseasvotefoundation.org) The Overseas Vote Foundation is a non-partisan organization that assists "overseas and military voters participate in federal elections." The organization's website has helpful tips, schedules, and links to assist overseas American Citizens, State Department employees, active duty military, and their families "within and outside the United States vote under the Uniformed and Overseas Citizens Absentee Voting Act (UOCAVA)."

Military Voter Protection Project: (www.mvpproject.org) The Military Voter Protection Project (MVP Project), is a program of The Legacy Foundation (www.legacyfoundation.us), a non-partisan organization. The MVP Project promotes and protects "military members' right to vote and ensuring that their votes are counted on Election Day. Utilizing media, education, and litigation, the MVP Project fights to ensure military voters have an opportunity to register, request an absentee ballot, and cast a vote regardless of their location in the world."

Get Out The Vet: (www.getoutthevet.org) Founded by the author, Get Out the Vet is recruiting veterans and their families to: work with counties, states, and military voter assistance officers to ensure our overseas military get timely registrations and ballots; dispatch veterans to monitor the election and report on suspicious votes and voter intimidation; and organize former JAG officers to prepare and file challenges to suspicious votes found. Why veterans? Every vet has sworn an oath to "preserve, protect, and defend the Constitution" and many have gone into harm's way to do so; vets understand rules of engagement and the chain of command and, given clear instructions, vets can be counted upon to act within the election laws; vets have gained the respect and admiration of our fellow Americans and will be credible witnesses to ensure a fair and fraud free election.

True the Vote: (www.truethevote.org) a national non-partisan organization growing out of the Tea Party movement in Texas, True the Vote "actively protect[s] the rights of legitimate voters, regardless of their political party affiliation." True the Vote's initiatives include: mobilizing and training volunteers as election monitors; pursuing fraud reports to ensure prosecution; creating documentaries and training videos; outreach to raise awareness of vote fraud; and programs to validate registration lists and detect errors. True the Vote has affiliates in a number of states.

Common Cause: (www.commonblog.com) it's not only Republicans that care about fair, fraud-free elections. Generally associated with Democratic Party positions, Common Cause is a non-partisan organization recruiting volunteers to poll watch in Democratic Primaries and other elections. Common Cause is testing a mobile app called Poll Watch USA to crowd source poll monitoring by allowing "voters to report polling place problems in real time."

State Poll Monitoring Organizations: Voters in nearly every state have set up organizations to get out the vote, research registration accuracy and provide election monitors and poll workers to ensure a fair and fraud free election. An example of one that had significant success during the recent 2012 recall election is We're Watching Wisconsin Elections:

(www.werewatchingwisconsinelections.org) A Republican-supported, non-partisan organization, We're Watching Wisconsin Elections played a significant role in ensuring that the 2012 Wisconsin recall election was fair and fraud free. The organization both trained and organized election observers and dispatched them to key polling places.

About the author

Ben Brink has over 30 years of experience in the management of high technology companies and in venture capital—in Silicon Valley, Southern California, and the Midwest, with operations in Europe and Asia. As CEO, he has led startup, early-stage, growth-stage, and mid-sized companies, both private and public in the software, defense electronics, medical electronics, environmental, and biotechnology market spaces. Recruited into the Federal Government in 2006, he turned around a $400M program, bringing the new biometric US passport into production. A Captain in the Navy Reserve, he was recalled to active duty in 2007, deploying to Afghanistan, where he led efforts to increase intelligence sharing and coordinate operations between

Afghanistan, Pakistan, and ISAF forces—awarded Bronze Star; following demobilization, Brink took command of Navy Intelligence Reserve Region Southwest, in San Diego. Retiring from the Navy at the beginning of 2011, he has re-established his corporate advisory practice, The McAlester Group, and is a founding partner in Carthage Intellectual Capital Management, a new firm that has developed novel valuation techniques and an investment vehicle to monetize productive intellectual property. Volunteer efforts include: Director Employment Initiative Program for the Missouri ESGR, and mentor and judge for the Washington University Skandalaris Center for Entrepreneurial Studies and the St. Louis IT Entrepreneurial Network. Brink holds degrees from: Harvard—MBA; Stanford—MS (Operations Research) and BS (Mathematics); and US Army War College—MS (Strategic Studies). Brink was the Republican nominee for the US House of Representatives for CA-14 in 1994 and 1996.

References

[1] Franklin, Benjamin, Poor Richard's Almanac, John Petrie's Collection of Benjamin Franklin Quotes, jpetrie.myweb.uga.edu/poor_richard.html

[2] Franklin, Benjamin, Benjamin Franklin, Wikipedia, 20 Aug 2012, en.wikipedia.org/wiki/Benjamin_Franklin

[3] Top 25 Quotes of Margaret Thatcher, Listverse, www.listverse.com/2007/12/21/top-25-quotes-of-margaret-thatcher

[4] Josef Stalin Vote Fraud Page, www.votefraud.org/josef_stalin_vote_fraud_page.htm

[5] Military Voter Protection Project, www.mvpproject.org

[6] Proof by assertion, Wikipedia, 24 July 2012, en.wikipedia.org/wiki/Proof_by_assertion

[7] Inaccurate, Costly, and Inefficient, Evidence that America's Voter Registration System Needs and Upgrade, The Pew Center on the States, February 2012

[8] Fox News Poll: Most think Voter ID laws are necessary, Fox News, 18 April 2012, www.foxnews.com/politics/2012/04/18/fox-news-poll-most-think-voter-id-laws-are-necessary

[9] Inaccurate, Costly, and Inefficient, Evidence that

America's Voter Registration System Needs and Upgrade, The Pew Center on the States, February 2012

[10] Pavlich, Katie, Finally: Florida Gains Access to DHS Database, Townhall, 15 August 2012, www.townhall.com/tipsheet/katiepavlich/2012/07/16/finally_florida_gains_access_to_dhs_database

[11] Shakespeare, William, Merchant of Venice (Launcelot Gobbo, Act II, Scene ii)

[12] Schaffer, Frederic Charles, "Elections For Sale: The Causes and Consequences of Vote Buying, Lynne Rienner Publisher, 30 January 2002

[13] Shawn, Eric, Widespread Vote buying in Eastern Kentucky Revealed, Fox News, 29 July 2012, foxnewsinsider.com/2012/07/29/widespread-vote-buying-in-eastern-kentucky-revealed/

[14] Stephens, John Paul, 2008, http://www.theprojectveritas.org/node/107

[15] Gumbel, Andrew, Steal This Vote: Dirty Elections and the Rotten History of Democracy in America, page 2

[16] Inaccurate, Costly, and Inefficient, Evidence that America's Voter Registration System Needs and Upgrade, The Pew Center on the States, February 2012

[17] Inaccurate, Costly, and Inefficient, Evidence that

America's Voter Registration System Needs and Upgrade, The Pew Center on the States, February 2012

[18] Presidential Elections, 1789-2008, www.infoplease.com/ipa/A0781450.html, Pearson Education, publishing as Infoplease, Copyright 2000–2012

[19] Inaccurate, Costly, and Inefficient, Evidence that America's Voter Registration System Needs and Upgrade, The Pew Center on the States, February 2012

[20] Examples Quotes, BranyQuote, www.brainyquote.com/quotes/keywords/examples.html

[21] Sivitek, Patrick, Dead Dog in Virginia Receives Voter Registration Forms, Huffington Post, 19 June 2012, www.huffingtonpost.com/2012/06/19/dead-dog-voter-registration-virginia_n_1609897.html

[22] Portnoy, Howard, Dead dog receives voter registration form; MSM blames 'Voter ID laws', examiner.com, 19 June 2012, www.examiner.com/article/dead-dog-receives-voter-registration-form-msm-blames-voter-id-laws

[23] Pappas, Alex, NH poll workers shown handing out ballots in dead peoples' names, The Daily Caller, 11 January 2012, www.dailycaller.com/2012/01/11/video-nh-poll-workers-shown-handing-out-ballots-in-dead-

peoples-names

24 Republican Disenfranchises Eric Holder, The other
    half or history, 15 April 2012,
    www.historyhalf.com/republican-disenfranchises-
    eric-holder/#more-3231

25 There's no excuse for voter fraud in WV, The State
    Journal, 20 June 2012,
    www.statejournal.com/story/18839126/theres-
    no-excuse-for-voter-fraud-in-wv

26 Welfare flap underscores differing approaches in
    Scott Brown-Elizabeth Warren Senate race,
    boston.com, 8 August 2012,
    www.boston.com/politicalintelligence/2012/08/0
    9/welfare-flap-underscores-differing-approaches-
    scott-brown-elizabeth-warren-senate-
    race/gPQICBypsML1g9H1fau7VO/story.html

27 Murphy, Julie, State tells election supervisors to cull
    dead voters, News Journal, 17 May 2012

28 Dead people voting, BallotPedia, 9 February 2012,
    www.ballotpedia.org/wiki/index.php/Dead_people
    _voting

29 Spakovsky, Hans A. Illegal Immigrants are Voting in
    the Amerian Elections, The Cutting Edge, 4
    August 2008

30 Piekarski, Jacob, Ellison: Voter ID Will Keep
    Snowplows off the Roads, Richfield Patch, 7
    August 2012,
    www.richfield.patch.com/articles/keith-ellison-

forum-on-voter-id-amendment-minnesota

[31] Public Law 107-252-Help America Voter Act of 2002, FDsys, US Government Printing Office, www.gpo.gov/fdsys/pkg/PLAW-107publ252/content-detail.html

[32] Porterfield, Mannix, The Register Herald, 17 November 2008

[33] Modernizing Voter Registration in New York, Brennan Center for Justice, www.brennancenter.org/page/-/Democracy/VRE/VRM%20NYS%20Reference%20Sheet.pdf

[34] Bauer & Potter, Voter Registration Is Key To Election Process, Washington Post, 25 June 2009

[35] Harris, Bev, 20% of All 18-year Olds Omitted -- Data Entry Failure for Last-Minute Registration Forms to Blame, BlackBoxVoting.org, 7 November 2011, www.bbvforums.org/cgi-bin/forums/board-profile.cgi?action=rate&topic=8&page=81772&post=58049

[36] Comstock-Gay, Stuart, Our Inadequate Patchwork Quilt of Registration Processes, Huffington Post, 4 November 2008, www.huffingtonpost.com/stuart-comstockgay/a-patchwork-quilt-of-regi_b_140871.html

[37] Bauer, Robert and Potter, Trevor, Voter Registration Is Key to Election Process, Washington Post, 25 June 2009, http://www.washingtonpost.com/wp-

dyn/content/article/2009/06/24/AR2009062403
095.html

[38] Comstock-Gay, Stuart, Our Inadequate Patchwork
Quilt of Registration Processes, Huffington Post, 4
November 2008, www.huffingtonpost.com/stuart-
comstockgay/a-patchwork-quilt-of-
regi_b_140871.html

[39] National Voter Turnout in Federal Elections: 1960-
2010, Pearson Education publishing as
Infoplease, 2000-2102,
www.infoplease.com/ipa/A0781453.html

[40] Voter turnout, Wikipedia, 23 July 2012,
en.wikipedia.org/wiki/Voter_turnout

[41] Heard, Andrew, Historical Voter Turnout in
Canadian Federal Elections & Referenda, 1867-
2008, Simon Fraser University, 2011,
www.sfu.ca/~aheard/elections/historical-
turnout.html

[42] Lijphart, Arend, Unequal Participation: Democracy's
Unresolved Dilemma, pp. 1–14, 16 American
Political Science Review, vol. 91, March 1997

[43] Wade Rathke, Wikipedia, 8 July 2012,
en.wikipedia.org/wiki/Wade_Rathke

[44] Fund, John, Stealing Elections: How Voter Fraud
Threatens our Democracy, 45-47, Encounter
Books (Kindle Edition) , Copyright 2004, 2008

[45] Ross, Lee, Supreme Court Refuses to Take ACORN

Case Appealing Fed Defunding, Fox News, 20 June 2011, www.foxnews.com/politics/2011/06/20/supreme-court-refuses-to-take-acorn-case-appealing-fed-defunding/

46 Arbitman , Marshall, ACORN files for Chapter 8 bankruptcy, CNN Politics, 2 Nov 2010, www.politicalticker.blogs.cnn.com/2010/11/02/acorn-files-for-chapter-7-bankruptcy

47 Fitten, Tom, Obama Administration Violating ACORN Funding Ban According to New Audit, Breitbart, 5 Dec 2011, www.breitbart.com/Big-Government/2011/12/05/Obama-Administration-Violating-ACORN-Funding-Ban-According-to-New-Audit

48 Former ACORN Director Gets $445 Mil From U.S. Treasury, Corruption Chronicles, Judicial Watch, June 7 2012, www.judicialwatch.org/blog/2012/06/former-acorn-director-gets-445-mil-from-u-s-treasury/

49 ACORN Offshoot Sues State For Not Registering Voters On Welfare, Corruption Chronicles, Judicial Watch, May 24 2012, www.judicialwatch.org/blog/2012/05/acorn-offshoot-sues-state-for-not-registering-voters-on-welfare/

50 Rotten ACORN, 2012, www.rottenacorn.com/activityMap.html

51 Fields, Michelle, Holder: Everyone knows 'in-person

voting fraud is uncommon', The Daily Caller, 12
June 2012,
www.dailycaller.com/2012/06/12/holder-
everyone-knows-in-person-voting-fraud-is-
uncommon-video/

[52] Video of the Week, The Foundry, 10 March, 2010,
blog.heritage.org/2010/03/10/video-of-the-week-
we-have-to-pass-the-bill-so-you-can-find-out-
what-is-in-it/

[53] Van Wanggaard recall, Wisconsin State Senate
(2012), Ballotpedia, 10 July 2012,
www.ballotpedia.org/wiki/index.php/Van_Wangg
aard_recall,_Wisconsin_State_Senate_(2012)

[54] Gonzalez, Rangel-Espaillat vote-count odyssey
continues, NY Daily News, 6 July 2012,
articles.nydailynews.com/2012-07-
06/news/32569607_1_poll-workers-district-
leaders-paper-ballots

[55] Malkin, Michelle, Bombshell in Wisconsin: Supreme
Court race swings to conservative Prosser, 7 April
2011,
www.michellemalkin.com/2011/04/07/bombshel
l-in-wisconsin-supreme-court-race-swings-to-
conservative-prosser/

[56] David Prosser, Jr., Wikipedia, 15 May 2012
en.wikipedia.org/wiki/David_Prosser,_Jr.#2011_R
e-election_campaign

[57] Spakovsky, Hans A., Voter Fraud is a Proven
Election Manipulation Tactic, Debate Club, US

News, 13 June 2012, www.usnews.com/debate-club/is-voter-fraud-a-real-problem/voter-fraud-is-a-proven-election-manipulation-tactic

[58] Bowes, Mark, VA investigates Voter Fraud, Richmond Times-Dispatch, 22 April 2012

[59] Minnesota Leads in the Nation in Voter Fraud Convictions, PR Newswire, 13 October 2011, www.prnewswire.com/news-releases/minnesota-leads-the-nation-in-voter-fraud-convictions-131782928.html?TC=CrowdFactory_Facebook&cf_from=http%3A%2F%2Fwww.prnewswire.com%2Fnews-releases%2Fminnesota-leads-the-nation-in-voter-fraud-convictions-131782928.html&cf_synd_id=xacDffv

[60] Fund, John, Stealing Elections: How Voter Fraud Threatens our Democracy, 101-105, Encounter Books (Kindle Edition) , Copyright 2004, 2008

[61] Election, BranyQuote, www.brainyquote.com/quotes/keywords/election_3.html

[62] Federal Court finds Obama appointees interfered with New Black Panther prosecution, Beltway Confidential, 30 July 2102, www.washingtonexaminer.com/federal-court-finds-obama-appointees-interfered-with-new-black-panther-prosecution/article/2503500

[63] FVAP.GOV, www.fvap.gov/faq.html#ocq7

[64] Military Winston Churchill Quotes,

www.quoteswinstonchurchill.com/military-quotes

[65] Inbody, Don Voting and the American Military, Don Inbody, CivMilBlog, 26 October 2011, www.civmilblog.com/2010/03/voting-and-american-military.html

[66] George B. McClellan, Wikipedia, 8 August 2012, en.wikipedia.org/wiki/George_B._McClellan

[67] Knight, Glenn B., Brief History of the Grand Army of the Republic, Sons of Union Veterans of the Civil War, www.suvcw.org/gar.htm

[68] Inbody, Don Voting and the American Military, Don Inbody, CivMilBlog, 26 October 2011, www.civmilblog.com/2010/03/voting-and-american-military.html

[69] Military Voting and the Law: Procedural and Technological Solutions to the Ballot Transit Problem, R. Michael Alvarez, Thad E. Hall, Brian E. Roberts, Institute of Public and International Affairs, The University of Utah, 8 Mar 2007

[70] Inbody, Don Voting and the American Military, Don Inbody, CivMilBlog, 26 October 2011, www.civmilblog.com/2010/03/voting-and-american-military.html

[7171] Inbody, Don Voting and the American Military, Don Inbody, CivMilBlog, 26 October 2011, www.civmilblog.com/2010/03/voting-and-american-military.html

[72] Inbody, Don Voting and the American Military, Don Inbody, CivMilBlog, 26 October 2011, www.civmilblog.com/2010/03/voting-and-american-military.html

[73] Inbody, Don Voting and the American Military, Don Inbody, CivMilBlog, 26 October 2011, www.civmilblog.com/2010/03/voting-and-american-military.html

[74] Truman, Harry S., Special Message to the Congress on Absentee Voting by Members of the Armed forces, Public Papers of Harry S. Truman, Truman Library, 22Aug 1949, www.trumanlibrary.org/publicpapers/index.php

[75] Wright, Samuel F., Captain, JAGC, USN (Ret.),The Scandal of Military Voter Disenfranchisement, PJ Media, 4 Nov 2010

[76] Post-Election Survey Reports, www.fvap.gov/reference/pesurveyrpts.html

[77] Help America Vote Act, Wikipedia, 2011, en.wikipedia.org/wiki/Help_America_Vote_Act

[78] Military and Overseas Voter Empowerment Act, Wikipedia, 2012, en.wikipedia.org/wiki/Military_and_Overseas_Voter_Empowerment_Act

[79] Eighteenth Report: 2008 Post Election Survey Report, Federal Voting Assistance Program, March 2011, www.fvap.gov/resources/media/18threport.pdf

[80] Nineteenth Report" 2010 Post Election survey report to CongressFederal Voting Assistance Program, , September 2011, www.fvap.gov/resources/media/2010report.pdf

[81] Overseas Voting—Challenges and Innovation, electionline.org Briefing, October 2007

[82] Overseas Vote Foundation, www.overseasvotefoundation.org/vote/home.htm

[83] NEW VOTER REGISTRATION AND BALLOT REQUEST NOW AVAILABLE, Federal Voting Assistance Program press release #28, 20 October 2011

[84] Counting Votes 2012: A State by State Look at Election Preparedness, Verified Voting Foundation, 2012, www.verifiedvoting.org

[85] Jackson, Ramon, The Military Absentee Vote, 27 Nov 2001, www.patriot.net/~eastlnd2/sv.htm

[86] Mazur, Diane H., The Bullying of America: A cautionary tale about civil-military relations and voting reform, University of Florida, 2005

[87] Military votes must count, Samuel F. Wright, The Washington Times, 15 December 2000

[88] Letter to President William J. Clinton from MG J. C. Pennington, USA (Ret.), President, National Association for Uniformed Services, 31 December 1996

[89] Could Obama Win the Military Vote?, New York

Times, 25 May 2012

[90] Whose Military Vote, Washington Post, 12 October 2004

[91] Spaulding, Pam, Out of 2 million military and overseas voters in 2010 only 4.6% of those votes counted, Pam's House Blend, www.pamshouseblend.firedoglake.com/2012/06/27/out-of-2-million-military-and-overseas-voters-in-2010-only-4-6-of-those-votes-counted, 27 June 2012

[92] Axelrod defends suit on Ohio military voting law, calls Romney's stance 'shameful', Fox News.com, 5 August 2012 www.foxnews.com/politics/2012/08/05/axelrod-defends-suit-on-ohio-military-voting-law-calls-romney-stance-hameful/#ixzz22yjm70Re

[93] Flynn, Mike, Flashback: Democrats Worked Hard to Disqualify Overseas Military Ballots in 2000, Recount, Breitbart TV, 6 August 2012, www.breitbart.com/Big-Government/2012/08/05/flashback-dems-disqualified-military-ballots-in-2000

[94] Sammon, William, Stiffing the troops serving overseas, Washington Times, National Weekly Edition, Volume 8, Number 20, 2001

[95] Drudge Report, November 2000

[96] George W. BUSH and Richard Cheney, Candidates for the Office of President and Vice President of

the United States, and The Republican Party of Florida, Plaintiffs, v. The HILLSBOROUGH COUNTY CANVASSING BOARD, et al., Defendants. No. 3:00-CV-533/LAC. United States District Court, N.D. Florida, Pensacola Division. 8 December 2000

[97] Help America Vote Act, Wikipedia, en.wikipedia.org/wiki/Help_America_Vote_Act

[98] Congressional Record, 107th Congress (2001-2002), STATEMENTS ON INTRODUCED BILLS AND JOINT RESOLUTIONS, 15 February 2001

[99] Feldstein, Mark, A half-century of political dirty tricks, The Washington Post, 14 Jan 2011, www.washingtonpost.com/wp-dyn/content/article/2011/01/13/AR2011011305693.html

[100] Fund, John, Stealing Elections: How Voter Fraud Threatens our Democracy,90-92, Encounter Books (Kindle Edition) , Copyright 2004, 2008

[101] Fund, John, Stealing Elections: How Voter Fraud Threatens our Democracy, 83, Encounter Books (Kindle Edition) , Copyright 2004, 2008

[102] The Florida Recount of 2000, FactCheck.org, 11 Nov 2001, www.factcheck.org/2008/01/the-florida-recount-of-2000/

[103] Fund, John, Stealing Elections: How Voter Fraud Threatens our Democracy, 69, Encounter Books (Kindle Edition) , Copyright 2004, 2008

104 The Truth About Fraud, Missouri 2000, Bennan
Center for Justice at NYU School of Law,
www.truthaboutfraud.org/case_studies_by_state/
missouri_2000.html

105 Fund, John, Stealing Elections: How Voter Fraud
Threatens our Democracy, 128-131, Encounter
Books (Kindle Edition) , Copyright 2004, 2008

106 Fund, John, Stealing Elections: How Voter Fraud
Threatens our Democracy, 131, Encounter Books
(Kindle Edition) , Copyright 2004, 2008

107 Bond Alleges Voter Fraud in Missouri, Online
NewsHour, KETC9, 9 November 2000,
www.pbs.org/newshour/updates/november00/ca
rnahan_11-9.html

108 Chain Voting, Douglas W. Jones, Black Box Voting,
26 Aug 2005, www.bbvdocs.org/reports/NIST-
Threats/ChainVoting.pdf

109 Creation of the Illinois State Board of Elections and
other Election Fraud Legislation, p 498, Depaul
Law Review, 1973-1974, www.heinonline.org

110 Reid, Joy-Ann, The cruel myth of voter fraud, The
Miami Herald, 11 July 2012,
www.miamiherald.com/2012/07/11/2891716/th
e-cruel-myth-of-voter-fraud.html

111 Hewitt, Hugh, If It's Not Close They Can't Cheat,
60-61, answers.google.com

112 Taylor, John H., Letter #13 – Face It: Nixon Really

Did Bow Out in '60, The Richard Nixon
Foundation, 28 November 2000,
letters.nixonfoundation.org/2000/11/28/letters-
from-yorba-linda-13-face-it-nixon-really-did-bow-
out-in-60/

[113] Mount Nixon: The Great Kennedy Disaster,
www.mountnixon.com/kennedy.

[114] Keen, Judy, Chicago ties cast shadow on 1960
presidential win, USA Today, 26 September 2010

[115] Stone, Roger, Did JFK Steal The 1960 Election?, 7
December 2010, The StoneZone,
www.stonezone.com/article.php?id=391

[116] Kusch, Brank, Battleground Chicago: The Police
and the 1968 Democratic National Convention,
University of Chicago Press, 1 May 2008

[117] Churchill, Military Quotes, www.military-
quotes.com/Churchill.htm

[118] Carter, Jimmy, Turning Point, page 205, Times
Books, 28 December 1993

[119] The Observation of the 1996 Nicaraguan Elections,
Latin American and Caribbean Program, The
Carter Center, Atlanta, GA, 1997

[120] Building Confidence in U.S. Elections, Report of the
Commission on Federal Election Reform, Center
for Democracy and Election Management,
American University, September 2005,
www1.american.edu/ia/cfer/

[121] Building Confidence in U.S. Elections, Report of the Commission on Federal Election Reform, page ii, Center for Democracy and Election Management, American University, September 2005, www1.american.edu/ia/cfer

[122] Fund, John, Stealing Elections: How Voter Fraud Threatens our Democracy, 150, Encounter Books (Kindle Edition) , Copyright 2004, 2008

[123] Building Confidence in U.S. Elections—Report of the Commission on Federal Election Reform, September 2005

[124] Building Confidence in U.S. Elections—Report of the Commission on Federal Election Reform, September 2005

[125] Building Confidence in U.S. Elections—Report of the Commission on Federal Election Reform, September 2005

[126] BranyQuote, Jan Brewer Quotes, www.brainyquote.com/quotes/authors/j/jan_brewer.html

[127] Justice Kennedy: Arizona Voter Registration Law OK for Now, 2012, The New media Journal, Arizona Daily Star, www.newmediajournal.us/indx.php/item/5920

[128] Fitzpatrick, Jack and Persad, Khara, Arizona and the feds clash – again – this time over voter registration, Green Valley News and Sun, 14 August 2012, www.gvnews.com/state/arizona-

and-the-feds-clash-again-this-time-over-
voter/article_a5901f94-e651-11e1-afcf-
001a4bcf887a.html

[129] Turner, Jim, Florida to DOJ: 'We Respectfully
Disagree', Sunshine State News, 6 June 2012

[130] Martel, Frances, Homeland Security Has Been
Stonewalling, CNN, 12 June 2012,
www.mediaite.com/tv/fl-gov-rick-scott-defends-
voter-registration-push-on-cnn-homeland-
security-has-been-stonewalling

[131] Martel, Frances, Homeland Security Has Been
Stonewalling, CNN, 12 June 2012,
www.mediaite.com/tv/fl-gov-rick-scott-defends-
voter-registration-push-on-cnn-homeland-
security-has-been-stonewalling

[132] Spakovsky, Hans von, The Problem of Non-Citizen
Voting, The Foundry, The Heritage Foundation,
Jul 20 2012, blog.heritage.org/2012/07/20/the-
problem-of-non-citizen-voting

[133] de Tocqueville, Alexis, Alexis de Tocqueville Quotes,
BrainyQuote,
www.brainyquote.com/quotes/authors/a/alexis_d
e_tocqueville.html

[134] Salam, Reihan, The Voter ID Conversation, The
Agenda, 25 July 2012,
www.nationalreview.com/agenda/312318/voter-
id-conversation-reihan-salam

[135] Spakovsky, Hans von and Ingram, Alex, Without

Proof: The Unpersuasive Case Against Voter identification, The Heritage Foundation, 24 August 2011, www.heritage.org/research/reports/2011/08/without-proof-the-unpersuasive-case-against-voter-identification

[136] Progress Report, Carter-Baker Commission on Federal Election Reform: Status of the Recommendations, Center for Democracy and Election Management, American University, September 2005—June 2007, www1.american.edu/ia/cdem/usp/np/cbc_progress_2007_06_12.pdf

[137] Spakovsky, Hans von and Ingram, Alex, Without Proof: The Unpersuasive Case Against Voter identification, The Heritage Foundation, 24 August 2011, www.heritage.org/research/reports/2011/08/without-proof-the-unpersuasive-case-against-voter-identification

[138] Lord, Jeffrey, Did Chris Matthews Participate in Voter Fraud?, The Spectacle Blog, The American Spectator, 27 Jun 2012 www.spectator.org/blog/2012/06/27/did-chris-matthews-participate

[139] Levy, Colin, Voter ID Standoff, The Wall Street Journal, 23 August 2012, online.wsj.com/article/SB10000872396390444270404577607160943756548.html

[140] Spakovski, Hans von and Beck, Katie, Lessons from

the Voter ID Experience in Kansas, The Heritage Foundation, July 25, 2012

[141] Spakovsky, Hans von, Lessons from the Voter ID Experience in Georgia, The Heritage Foundation,19 March 2012

[142] Panel debating the pros and cons of new voter registration laws, American Bar Association, August 2012, www.abanow.org2012/08

[143] Rooney, Thomas J., Federal Judge Upholds Actions to Prevent Voter Fraud, 6 June 2012, Congressman Thomas J. Rooney official website, rooney.house.gov/index.php?option=com_content&view=article&id=3415:rooney-federal-judge-upholds-actions-to-prevent-voter-fraud&catid=50:2012-press-releases

[144] Thompson, Fred, Tweet, @fredthompson, 7 June 2012

[145] Nichols, John, Recall Campaign Against Scott Walker Fails, John, Nation, 5 June 2012, www.thenation.com/blog/168242/recall-campaign-against-scott-walker-fails#

[146] We're Watching Wisconsin Elections, www.werewatchingwisconsinelections.org

[147] Trinko, Katrina, National Review Online, 8 June 2012, www.nationalreview.com/articles/302180/winning-wisconsin-ground-game-katrina-trinko

[148] BranyQuote, Election Quotes,
www.brainyquote.com/quotes/keywords/election_3.html

[149] The Wizard of Oz, Metro-Goldwin-Mayer, 1939

[150] Fund, John, Stealing Elections: How Voter Fraud
Threatens our Democracy, 156-157, Encounter
Books (Kindle Edition) , Copyright 2004, 2008

[151] www.earc.berkeley.edu.general-intro.php

[152] Sanctis, Matt, Springfield News-Sun Friday Feb 17,
2012 Matt Sanctis

[153] www.commonblog.com

[154] www.moprecinctproject.org

[155] Reagan, Ronald, The Quotations Page,
www.quotationspage.com/quotes/Ronald_Reagan

[156] Voter Identification Requirements, National
Conference of State Legislatures, 2012,
www.ncsl.org/legislatures-elections/elections/voter-id.aspx

[157] Goodreads, Quotes About Voting,
www.goodreads.com/quotes/tag/voting?auto_login_attempted=true

www.ingramcontent.com/pod-product-compliance
Lightning Source LLC
LaVergne TN
LVHW051521080426
835509LV00017B/2155